WINNING WAYS
WITH CHEESE

Cheesemaking

The Author would like to thank
the following for their kind
help and co-operation

Portraits of the prizewinners
and Mary Berry by **Christine Murray**

Jacket photograph by **Paul Kemp**

Text photographs by **Sue Jorgensen**

Engraving of 18th Century cheesemaking
reproduced by permission of the **Radio Times
Hulton Picture Library**

Engraving of the first cheese factory
reproduced by permission of the **Institute
of Agricultural History and Museum of English
Rural Life**

Food preparation by **Moya Maynard**

Photographic accessories

Habitat
206 Kings Road, London SW3
and throughout UK, France,
Belgium and USA

The General Trading Company
144 Sloane Street, London SW1

The Craftsmen Potters Shop
Marshall Street, London W1

Tridias
Richmond: Bath: Dartington

Toys
97 Walton Road, East Molesey,
Surrey

Designed and illustrated by **Tony Streek**

Published 1983 on behalf of the English
Country Cheese Council by **Purnell
Publishers Ltd**

© Copyright **The English Country Cheese Council**

Typesetting and Make-up by
Quadraset Ltd
Radstock, Bath, Avon

Printed in Great Britain by
Hazell Watson & Viney
Aylesbury, Bucks

ISBN 0 361 05908 6

WINNING WAYS WITH CHEESE

Purnell

Contents

The recipes selected from the competition entries have been re-written to provide uniformity throughout the book.

PRIZEWINNERS OF THE ENGLISH COUNTRY CHEESE
COUNCIL'S COMPETITION 'MAKE YOUR MARK WITH
ENGLISH CHEESE' AT THE HOUSE OF COMMONS

The rosette denotes the chapter winner's recipe

From left to right (back row): Cecily Lake, Valerie Wareham,
Paul Carmody, Pat Austin, Barbara Briggs

From left to right (front row): Isabel Gregory, Nicola
Solomons, Carolann Bowers, Pam Marchant

Foreword by *Mary Berry.*

As one of the judges of the 'Make Your Mark With English Cheese' competition, I was amazed by the tremendous variety of recipes and hints submitted by good cooks from all over the country.

There were over 14,000 entries, all of a very high standard. I would not have been too surprised if most of the recipes featured that staunch old favourite, English Cheddar, but I was, in fact, delighted to discover that the competitors used all nine of the regional English cheeses, to delicious effect. With so many original ideas to choose from, the judges' criterion when selecting the prize-winners was: 'Would I serve it to my family, and would they like it?'.

The nine regional English cheeses are: Caerphilly, English Cheddar, Cheshire, Derby, Double Gloucester, Lancashire, Leicester, Stilton and Wensleydale, each with its own distinctive flavour and character. As a first-rate source or protein, they really are wonderful value for money.

Here are just a few of my own ideas for serving English cheeses. Why not 'go French' on occasions, and serve cheese before the pudding? Offer only two or three cheeses, but present them attractively by decorating the cheese board with vine leaves, blackcurrant leaves or other fruit leaves from the garden and perhaps a small bunch of grapes too.

Cheese with apple is a firmly-established favourite, but have you tried serving English cheeses with peaches, dessert plums or damsons?

You can probably think of a few more variations. It's surprising how simple ideas like these can transform what was just 'the cheese into something rather special.

Try adding crumbled Sage Derby to a stuffing for pork or Double Gloucester with chives to a cheesy sauce with fish. English cheeses are all marvellous in sauces, in dips or baked potatoes . . . in Welsh rarebit, or simply toasted under the grill — extra delicious with sliced tomato underneath. If you want a golden brown topping quickly dust the grated cheese with paprika just before grilling.

I like to grate English cheese over hot cooked green vegetables, or potatoes. The same treatment lends zest to green salad.

If you have some hard cheese left over, try potted cheese: made from grated cheese, mashed with thick mayonnaise, ground black pepper, and crushed garlic, with fresh chopped chives or parsley as a topping.

But don't forget how good and nutritious English cheeses are when eaten just as they are — cubed for parties, an anytime snack with celery or biscuits. Accompanied by crusty bread and pickle, English cheese is a satisfying meal in itself.

The storage of cheese is important. Wrapped in cling film and kept in the refrigerator, it will remain in perfect condition for a week. After that time, it is best grated, or stored in the freezer. Remember hard cheeses freeze best — the higher the fat content, the better. You may find that freezing makes the cheese a little crumbly if kept in the freezer for more than a couple of weeks but it should taste just as good.

There's no end to the versatility of this valuable food. If you've been taking cheese for granted, then perhaps it's time you tasted some new varieties of English cheese. Try them all! One of the less familiar could well become your family's favourite.

Cheese

Cheese has a beauty and attractiveness entirely of its own. It has distinctive characteristics and needs to be treated carefully both by those who make it and those who eat it, in order to gain the maximum enjoyment from each particular aroma and flavour.

It is frequently enjoyed just by itself or with beer or wine; it is important in the kitchen as an ingredient to simple wholesome dishes and in highly refined cuisine; it has a traditional place on the table, in fact it is almost indispensable.

There are nine traditional English cheeses which offer a variety of flavours and textures for eating and cooking. There are also many new English cheeses with interesting flavours to tempt the more sophisticated palate.

Cheese is not only tasty and very nutritious but also very good value for money.

Cheesemaking in 1768

The Cheese Story

Cheese has been made for over 2000 years and the Greeks even appointed a god for it (Aristaeus, son of Apollo).

Legend has it that it was discovered, accidentally, by nomadic Arab tribesmen in the desert. They carried ewe's milk in a bag made from a dried sheep's stomach. When they slit the bag open after a long days travelling in the desert, it was found to contain not milk but a sour curd-like substance, the most primitive form of cheese. Heat from the sun had turned the milk sour and rennin in the dried sheep's stomach had curdled the milk, turning it to curds and whey.

It was the Greeks who gave cheese its present day French and Italian names. The French 'fromage' and the Italian 'formaggio' derive from the Greek 'formos' — wicker basket which the ancient Greeks used for draining their cheese.

The Romans called these baskets 'caseus' from which comes the German 'kase', the Dutch 'kaas', the Spanish 'queso', the Portuguese 'quiejo', and the Anglo-Saxon 'cese' or 'cyse', from which eventually evolved the word 'cheese'. The making of cheese has hardly changed since those days long ago. Today, whether the final product is hard or soft, strong or mild, it all starts off in the same way as the ancient product: as coagulated or curdled milk.

Farmhouse cheese continued being made up until the outbreak of the second World War, but the war years put an abrupt end to cheese variety as governmental policy required the uniform production of a mild Cheddar in all farmhouses and creameries throughout the country. The aim of these restrictions was to provide large quantities of a nourishing food. It was not until post war-time food rationing ended in the early 1950's that the individuality, taste and textures of our traditional cheeses were re-discovered when both Farmhouse and Creamery production began again.

In England and Wales cheese-making remained a purely farmhouse activity until well into the 19th century. Then, in 1860, English cheese-making was hit by a disaster. Cattle disease killed off thousands of animals, and the milk yield dropped drastically. This caused a shortage of cheese and allowed an influx of American 'Cheddar type' cheese to swamp the English market.

To prevent this, the English cheese-makers decided to preserve their traditional varieties by opening factories where larger quantities of cheese of a consistent quality could be produced. The first cheese factory, or more properly named 'creamery', was opened at Derby in 1870. By 1875, Derbyshire had six cheese creameries and others had opened in Cheshire, Staffordshire, Gloucestershire, Somerset and Leicestershire.

The first cheese factory was opened in Derby in 1870

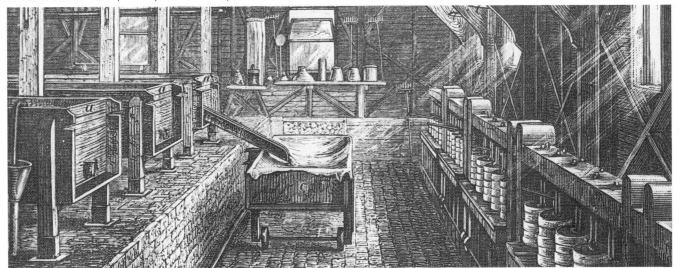

Cheesemaking

Although cheese comes in a wide variety of textures, colours and flavours, all cheeses go through the same fundamental steps during their manufacture. These are:

1 souring and ripening the milk

2 setting or coagulating the milk

3 cutting or breaking the curds

4 scalding the curds

5 draining the whey

6 milling

7 salting

8 pressing the curd

9 maturing

The traditional method of making Cheddar cheese, begins with the heating of full fat milk to 73°C (164°F). It is then cooled to 30°C (86°F), starter (harmless bacteria which increase the acidity of the milk by turning the lactose to lactic acid) is added, and after about 35 minutes the acidity is sufficient for rennet to be added, and it is thoroughly stirred into the milk. It is the rennet that coagulates the milk.

It is then cooled to 30°C (86°F) and a starter is added

About 45 minutes later the curd is solid enough to be cut into small particles with special knives to release the whey. The curds and whey are heated to 39°C (102°F), and stirred continuously. This process is known as 'scalding' the curd, during which time the acidity increases and the curd particles shrink as the whey exudes from them.

The curd is solid enough to be cut into small particles with special knives

When the correct acidity is reached, the curd is allowed to settle to the bottom of the vat and the whey is drawn off. The curd is then cut into blocks and turned regularly for about 2 hours either in the vat or on racks. This is known as the **cheddaring process** and allows the correct acidity and dryness to develop.

The curd is then cut into blocks

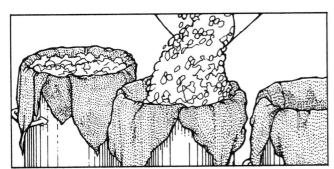

This mixture is then put into course linen cloth-lined moulds and pressed down firmly

The curd is then milled (cut into little pieces), and salted (approximately 2 per cent salt). The salt is thoroughly mixed into the curd to improve the flavour and keeping qualities. This mixture is then put into coarse linen cloth-lined moulds and pressed down firmly. The moulds are put into a mechanical press which expels more whey and causes the curd to adhere together. This pressing period can last from 24—48 hours and during this time the cheese is turned and the cloth changed.

It is finally taken to the storage room where it remains at a set degree of humidity and temperature

After pressing, the cheese is released from the mould. The rind is covered with a protective cloth, then waxed to prevent drying out and finally taken to the storage room where it remains at a set degree of humidity and temperature. The cheese now begins to ripen (mature) and acquire its own individuality.

All the other traditional English cheese are made by the same process, but variations in the temperature and time the milk is left to ripen; the acidity levels and size of the curds when first cut and the time of pressing – all contribute to the wide variety of cheeses available.

Creamery cheeses follow a similar method of production but much of the labour intensive aspects such as cutting the curds is mechanised as the quantities of milk used for manufacturing

Much of the labour-intensive aspects are mechanised

cheese is so much larger than the smaller farmhouse cheese-maker. For ease of storage and cutting most creameries specialise in block-formed rather than round cheeses which are covered in special air free vacuum wrapping instead of the traditional wax bandage.

Most creameries specialise in block-formed rather than round cheeses

Blue cheeses such as Blue Stilton, Blue Cheshire and Blue Wensleydale follow the same basic cheese-making steps but can only be made in the traditional shapes. The blue comes from a harmless blue mould culture that is added to the milk during manufacture. The blue veins appear after the cheeses have been pieced by metal prongs to create air holes which allow the blue mould to develop naturally in the cheese.

The nine varieties of English and Welsh Cheese

Caerphilly

Originally a Welsh cheese from the Glamorgan village of the same name. The miners of Caerphilly were particularly fond of it because it remained moist when they took it down the mine. Also a wedge was just the right size for them to get their hands around, therefore only getting coal dust on the rind! This could be discarded after eating the dust-free cheese.

It is a semi-hard, smooth white cheese which ripens in about 2 weeks. The texture is close and moist but somewhat flaky, and it has a mild flavour, faintly salty, with a slightly acidic taste.

Cheshire

The oldest of the English cheeses, known in Roman Britain, mentioned in the Domesday book and was a favourite at the court of Queen Elizabeth I in the 16th Century.

Originally it was made on Cheshire farms and the rich natural salt deposits in the soil gave the cheese its distinctive tangy flavour. Cheshire cheese is now made throughout the cheese-producing areas of England and Wales.

There are three varieties, red, white and blue of which blue is the rarest. The red colour comes from a natural food colouring called annatto which is obtained from the berries of a South American shrub. Prior to the use of annatto, English cheeses were coloured with natural dyes such as carrot juice!

Both the red and the white cheeses are matured for about 6 weeks and have a characteristic loose, crumbly texture and a mellow flavour with a hint of saltiness.

Blue Cheshire is only made on the farm and matures for up to 2–3 months. It has a more creamy texture and the rich flavour characteristics of a blue cheese.

Derby

A moist but firm-textured cheese with a delicate flavour. The small production of Derby makes it one of the rarest of the English cheeses. It is pale honey coloured and matures for 4–6 weeks or more.

Sage Derby, once a traditional Christmas cheese, is now available all year round. Rubbed sage leaves are added to the curd before pressing which gives a green marbling effect to the cheese. It is matured for 3–4 months and has a pronounced flavour of sage.

Double Gloucester

The word 'double' refers to the traditional sizes of this cheese. It was originally made in two sizes, 'single' being half as big as the 'double'. When the 'single' went out of production the word 'double' was still retained.

It is a golden, straw-coloured cheese, which matures for at least 3 months. It has a full mellow taste with a creamy feel on the tongue. Annatto is added to give the attractive colour.

English Cheddar

Since the 16th century Cheddar has traditionally been made in the Mendip hills, close to Cheddar Gorge, in Somerset. It is now made in creameries in several parts of the country although Farmhouse Cheddars are still made only in the West Country. Over the centuries it was the West Country farmers who took the Cheddar cheese-making recipe with them when they emigrated to the new worlds of Canada, USA and New Zealand.

Today, there is a wide variation in flavour from mild to well matured. Mild Cheddar is generally sold after maturing from 3–5 months. English Cheddar should be at least 5 months old before it is sold as mature and is often best matured for 9–12 months. It has a close texture and varies in colour from pale cream to deep yellow.

Lancashire

Traditionally Lancashire was made only in its native county. It is a soft white crumbly cheese with a mild flavour when young. If allowed to mature for longer than the usual 8 weeks a full piquant flavour results.

The Farmhouse Lancashire is unusual amongst the English cheeses because one batch of curd is made during the evening and kept overnight, then added to freshly made curds the next morning. Some farmhouses still make a **Sage Lancashire** for Christmas.

Nowadays, most Lancashire cheese made in creameries has similar characteristics to the traditional Lancashire but, like other English cheeses, is made from a single batch of curd giving a mild flavoured crumbly cheese with a drier texture.

Leicester

A rich russet-red cheese, coloured with annatto. It is the brightest of all the English cheeses. Matured from 8–12 weeks, it is open-textured and has a mellow flavour. If kept longer it will develop a more nutty flavour.

Blue Stilton

Referred to as the 'King of English Cheeses' and regarded not only as a great English cheese but as one of the great cheeses of all time. A Certification Trade Mark ensures that it is made only in seven creameries situated in Leicestershire, Nottinghamshire and Derbyshire, using an old established method.

Originating in the 18th Century this blue cheese was named after the village called Stilton where it was first sold to the travellers on the Great North Road from London to York.

The cheese is creamy white in colour with blue veins radiating out from the centre and a rough natural crinkly brown crust. After maturing for 3–5 months Stilton has a rich, creamy flavour that is renowned by cheese lovers throughout the world. A young Stilton sold after only 3–4 weeks maturing is still white with a fresh mild flavour and open texture. This is known as **White Stilton**.

Wensleydale

Wensleydale cheese was originally made from ewe's milk by the monks who came to England with William the Conqueror and built Jervaulx Abbey in North Yorkshire. Having fled from the destruction of their Abbey by Henry VIII in the 15th Century the monks left a cheese-making recipe behind that was carried on by the local farmers with cows milk.

Matured for 3 weeks it has a fairly close texture but is crumbly with a mild, slightly sweet flavour that has a delicious honeyed after-taste.

The blue-veined variety is rare and has a close, soft texture with a rich creamy taste and is matured for about 6 months.

New English Cheeses

These cheeses have derived from traditional flavour combinations, for example cheese and pickle, cheese and onion. They are becoming increasingly easier to obtain, prepacked from supermarkets or cut from a round in cheese shops and cheese counters.

Any of these cheeses makes an interesting, attractive and unusual addition to the cheese board. A talking point for any occasion.

Cotswold

A tangy blend of Double Gloucester with chopped chives and onions.

Huntsman

Sometimes called the 'E' shaped cheese because of the unusual way in which the layers of Stilton and Double Gloucester are formed.

Charnwood or Applewood

Smoked Cheddar cheese with an attractive outer coating of paprika.

Sherwood

A blend of two traditional companions, Double Gloucester and sweet mixed pickle.

Windsor Red

Cheddar marbled with elderberry wine.

Rutland

An unusual mixture of Cheddar cheese, beer, garlic and parsley.

Walton

A blend of Cheddar and Blue Stilton coated in walnuts. A tasty cheese with an interesting texture.

Nutwood

An exciting blend of Cheddar cheese, roasted hazelnuts, raisins and cider.

Cheviot

A mild cheese consisting of a mixture of Cheddar cheese and chopped chives.

Ilchester

A blend of Double Gloucester with mustard pickle.

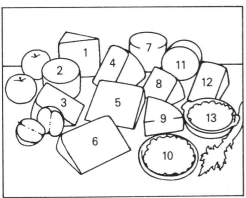

1 Cotswold
2 Cheviot
3 Charnwood or Applewood
4 Ilchester
5 Windsor Red
6 Huntsman
7 Nutwood
8 Walton
9 Lymeswold
10 Cream Cheese
11 Sherwood
12 Rutland
13 Cottage Cheese

Soft Cheeses

Soft cheeses have a high moisture content and are soft to the touch.

Unripened Soft Cheeses

The unripe soft cheeses are marked according to the fat content: full fat, medium fat, low fat and skimmed milk. In addition, cream cheese and double cream cheese are also available having a minimum fat content of 45 and 65 per cent respectively.

All unripened soft cheeses have a limited shelf life and are best eaten within a few days of manufacture.

Cottage Cheese is a low fat soft cheese made from skimmed milk. A cream dressing is added at the end of the manufacture resulting in a fat content of between 2% and 10%. The characteristic texture is controlled by the slow heating of the curd before washing and draining. Cottage cheese is also available with added flavours such as pineapple, ham or chives.

Ripened Soft Cheese

Lymeswold is the first soft blue cheese to be produced commercially in this country. As with all cheese, its flavour develops greatly and so look for the 'best before' date. Lymeswold is sold when it is still relatively young.

Storing Cheese

Freshly cut cheese should look fresh with no dried areas or beads of fat on the surface. Cut, pre-wrapped cheese should have no evidence of mould, moisture or greasiness inside the packing. If there is, it has been stored at too high a temperature.

Vacuum-packed cheese will keep longer than loosely-wrapped cheese, and the date codes of prepacked cheese is a good indication as to the optimum length of time to keep the cheese once you have bought it.

Cheese Storage

The length of time cheese will keep in good eating condition depends on it being kept well wrapped, and cool, as well as on the type of cheese. All cheese keeps best when stored between 5 to 7°C (40–45°F).

English Cheddar, Double Gloucester and Stilton will keep well in the refrigerator for as long as a month, providing the cheese is in good condition when purchased and is wrapped properly in cling film or foil. Younger cheeses should be eaten within a few days of buying.

Freshly cut or vacuum-packed cheese which has been opened, should be wrapped in cling film or foil. Close wrapping keeps the cheese moist and protects it from absorption of flavours from other foods.

Cheese should always be removed from the refrigerator at least one hour before serving to allow the flavour to return to normal.

Freezing Cheese

Younger, mild cheeses lose flavour during freezing, but the more mature cheeses can be kept in the freezer for about 3 months. As the salt in cheese may pit the foil the cheese should be wrapped in cling film and then foil, or put into freezer bags. Blocks of cheese for freezing should weigh no more than 450g (lb). Ideally, freeze in quantities you would normally use eg 100g (4oz) or 225g (8oz). Cheese is best thawed in the refrigerator overnight, leaving the wrapping on. The rind of blue cheese will always soften on thawing.

The Goodness of Cheese

Cheese can make a valuable contribution to the diet by providing generous amounts of protein, calcium and vitamin A.

The protein in cheese is of high quality, in that it provides essential amino acids in sufficient amounts to meet the body's requirements for maintenance and growth, of body tissues. Cheese is especially important for children because of its high calcium content which helps form strong bones and teeth, and it can easily be introduced into the diet from 6 months of age.

Elderly people also benefit from cheese, as a concentrated form of essential nutrients.

A balanced diet is essential for the growth and health of your family.
Just choose from each food group shown within the wheel – every day

Start here

FOODS FOR ACTIVITY AND WARMTH

FOODS FOR GROWTH AND REPAIR

FOODS FOR GENERAL GOOD HEALTH

Making the most of Cheese

One of the best things about cheese is its versatility. It can be included in any meal. Serve cheese with toast or eggs for breakfast, in flans, savouries and salads for lunch, as a garnish for soups and vegetables at dinner. Mild and soft cheeses can be used in mousses and soufflés for desserts. Any of the English cheeses can be included on a cheeseboard or eaten as a snack at anytime.

Cooking Cheese

Cheese is easy to prepare, just slice or grate it, but when used in cooking, it requires careful handling. Too much cooking causes the cheese to become leathery and unpalatable. Therefore only heat it very gently and always remove a sauce from the heat before stirring in the cheese. Hard cheese cooks best if it is first shredded or grated.

As cheese contains salt, dishes containing cheese need less salt adding to them, so great care should be taken when seasoning cheese dishes.

Cheeseboards

When preparing a cheese board, it is best to use two or three good size wedges rather than several small pieces of cheese. The selection of the cheese is important; it should provide a variety of colours, textures and flavours. Cheddar, Wensleydale and Blue Stilton make an interesting combination as do Double Gloucester, Sage Derby and Caerphilly.

When serving a round Stilton take a horizontal slice and then cut that into a wedge shaped segment – 'cut high, cut low, cut level'. This can be applied to any large piece of cheese served, but if served as a wedge try to maintain the wedge shape rather than cutting off the nose!

The cheeses should ideally be served with a small selection of fruit or celery sticks and biscuits or fresh crusty bread. Try serving the cheese board before the pudding, particularly if wine is being served with the meal, so the wine served with the main course can also be drunk with cheese.

Characteristics and Uses

It is advisable to buy only enough cheese for about a week at a time. However, for a large family or a party it may be more economical and convenient to buy a quarter, half or whole cheese, particularly if you have suitable storage space in the refrigerator or cool larder.

Caerphilly
Age when ready for eating – 2 weeks
Colour – white
Texture – close
Flavour – clean, mild and slightly salty
Characteristics and uses – especially good for tea with celery and thin slices of bread and butter

Cheshire
Age when ready for eating – 6 weeks
Colour – orange-red or white
Texture – loose and crumbly
Flavour – mild, mellow and slightly salted
Characteristics and uses – delicious combined with fruit, and even cake and biscuits. Blue Cheshire – a blue veined cheese, is sometimes available.

Derby
Age when ready for eating – 4–6 weeks or more
Colour – often honey coloured
Texture – buttery and open
Flavour – clean and tangy
Characteristics and uses – goes well with grapes, pears and apples. Sage Derby – flavoured with rubbed sage leaves – is a Christmas favourite.

Double Gloucester
Age when ready for eating – 3–4 months
Colour – golden, straw-coloured
Texture – buttery and open
Flavour – delicate and creamy
Characteristics and uses – excellent accompaniment to a pint of ale, or fresh fruit salad and fresh cream.

English Cheddar
Age when ready for eating – 3 months or more
Colour – pale cream to deep yellow
Texture – close
Flavour – clean, mellow and nutty
Characteristics and uses – most famous cheese of all, ideal for a variety of uses, but goes especially well with fruit and cider.

Lancashire
Age when ready for eating – 4–8 weeks or more.
Colour – white
Texture – soft, crumbly
Flavour – clean and mild
Characteristics and uses – excellent toasting properties, also for crumbling over soups and hotpots.

Leicester
Age when ready for eating – 8–12 weeks
Colour – rich russet-red
Texture – buttery and open
Flavour – mild and mellow
Characteristics and uses – good dessert cheese, but also excellent used in Welsh Rarebit.

Blue Stilton
Age when ready for eating – 3–5 months
Colour – blue vein
Texture – soft and close
Flavour – rich, mellow creamy
Characteristics and uses – the 'King of Cheeses'. Traditionally accompanied by port. White Silton is a young mild, crumbly cheese.

Wensleydale
Age when ready for eating – 3 weeks
Colour – white
Texture – fairly close
Flavour – clean, mild and slightly sweet
Characteristics and uses – goes well with crisp, juicy apples and apple pie. Blue Wensleydale is a blue veined cheese.

Weights and Measures for Cooks

Dry weight

Approximate gram (g) conversion to nearest round figure	Recommended gram (g) conversion to nearest 25g	Imperial ounce (oz)
28	25	1
57	50	2
85	75	3
113	100–125g	4 (¼ lb)
142	150	5
170	175	6
198	200	7
227	225	8 (½ lb)
255	250	9
284	300	10
311	325	11
340	350	12 (¾ lb)
368	375	13
396	400	14
425	425	15
453	450	16 (1lb)

Liquid measures

Approximate millilitre (ml) conversion to nearest round figure	Recommended millilitre (ml) equivalent	Imperial pint	Imperial fluid ounce (fl oz)
568	575–600	1	20
284	300	½	10
142	150	¼	5

Oven temperature chart

°C	°F	Gas Number	Description
110	225	¼	Very slow
130	250	½	Very slow
140	275	1	Slow
150	300	2	Slow
170	325	3	Moderate
180	350	4	Moderate
190	375	5	Moderately hot
200	400	6	Moderately hot
220	425	7	Hot
230	450	8	Hot
240	475	9	Very hot

The above oven temperature chart is a guide only and gives recommended equivalent settings, not exact conversions. To be absolutely sure of good results, always refer to your own cooker instruction book.

Temperatures for storage

Standard temperature for freezing − 18°C (0°F)
Standard temperature for refrigeration 5°C (41°F)
✳ Frozen food will keep up to one week
✳✳ Frozen food will keep up to four weeks
✳✳✳ Frozen food will keep up to three months
Only if the compartment has the following symbol
✳✳✳ as the rating should you attempt to freeze your own food. In addition the three stars illustrate the ability to store commercially frozen foods for up to 3 months

In all recipes in this book the ingredients are shown in both metric and imperial measures. However, the metric quantities are not exact conversions but calculated to give proportionately correct measurements for successful results

Where eggs are used in recipes, we suggest size 3 eggs are used

Soups and Starters

Homemade soups can be made as an appetiser or a meal in itself. With a cheese soup, the variety of texture, colour and flavour depends on your choice of cheese. Take care when adding the cheese to the hot liquid. The best results come by stirring in the finely grated cheese at the end of the cooking time and just before serving, reheat to just below boiling point, as overcooking will spoil the texture. The addition of a generous sprinkling of grated cheese makes a meal out of any soup.

Cubed, grated, sliced or crumbled, the combination of cheese with fruits, vegetables, sauces and dressings sets the scene for the meal to come. Many starters can be adapted for informal parties, barbecues and with a double portion – a meal in itself!

 ## Blue Stilton, Walnut and Grape Charlotte

4–6 thick slices of white bread, with crusts removed
100g (4oz) English butter
2 eggs, separated
salt and freshly ground pepper
¼ level teaspoon dry mustard
150ml (¼ pint) milk
15g (½oz) gelatine
175g (6oz) Blue Stilton, crumbled
100g (4oz) white grapes, skinned, pipped and quartered
50g (2oz) walnuts, chopped
150ml (5 fl oz) fresh double cream
a few extra walnut halves (optional)
black and green stuffed olives (optional)
parsley sprigs

1 Cut each slice of bread into four fingers. Melt the butter in a frying pan and fry the bread fingers in it until golden brown, turning once during cooking to brown both sides. Drain on absorbent kitchen paper

2 Use the bread fingers to line the sides of a 15cm (6 inch) charlotte mould or deep cake tin. Reserve a slice for the top

3 Beat the egg yolks in a basin with the salt and pepper to taste and mustard until pale and creamy

4 Bring the milk to the boil, then remove from the heat and pour over the yolk mixture, whisking continuously

5 Stand the basin over a saucepan of gently simmering water and cook, stirring continuously, until the mixture thickens enough to coat the back of a spoon. Do not allow the pan of water to boil, or overcook the mixture, as the egg yolks will curdle

6 Place 2 tablespoons cold water in a small bowl and sprinkle in the gelatine. Stand the bowl over a saucepan of hot water and heat gently until dissolved

7 Stir the gelatine into the cooked custard, then stir in the cheese, grapes and walnuts. Leave to cool and half set

8 Lightly whip the fresh cream until softly stiff, then carefully fold into the custard mixture using a metal spoon. Whisk the egg whites until stiff and fold into the custard mixture

9 Pour the mixture into the bread-lined mould or tin and finish with the reserved slice, chill until set

10 To serve, stand the mould in hot water for a few seconds, quickly wipe the outside and invert on to a serving dish or plate

11 Arrange the halved walnuts and olives around the charlotte and place olives and parsley on the service plate. Serve with Melba Toast

Serves 8

Blue Stilton, Walnut and Grape Charlotte

Cheese Soufflé with Fillets of Plaice

4 fillets plaice, skinned
salt and pepper
4 eggs, separated
75g (3oz) English Cheddar cheese, finely grated
parsley sprigs

1 Roll up the fish, season with salt and pepper and place in a well buttered 1 litre (2 pint) soufflé dish and cover

2 Bake 180°C (350°F), mark 4, for 5 minutes. Discard any liquid

3 Place the egg yolks in a basin and beat in the cheese

4 Whisk the egg whites until stiff, and gently fold into the cheese mixture. Pour over the fish

5 Bake 220°C (425°F), mark 7, for 12 to 15 minutes until well risen. Serve immediately, garnished with parsley

Serves 4

Mrs J. Hayter · Littlehampton

Charnwood Smoked Pâté with Almonds

100g (4oz) full fat soft cheese
100g (4oz) low fat soft (curd) cheese
150ml (5 fl oz) fresh double cream
15g (½oz) English butter
¼ level teaspoon chilli powder
¼ level teaspoon dried chervil
1 level teaspoon mustard powder
100g (4oz) whole blanched almonds
100g (4oz) Charnwood smoked Cheddar cheese
parsley sprigs

1 Cream the soft cheeses together. Lightly whip the fresh cream and fold into the cheese mixture; set aside

2 Melt the butter in a frying pan on very low heat and add the chilli powder, chervil and mustard powder. Cook for ½ minute

3 Reserve a few of the almonds for garnish and finely chop the remainder. Add to the frying pan with the Charnwood cheese then stir until just melted

4 Take the pan off the heat and mix thoroughly. Allow to cool slightly, then add to the creamed cheeses and stir through lightly

5 Divide the mixture between six ramekin dishes and chill until set

6 Toast reserved almonds. Garnish with the almonds and parsley sprigs and serve with toast fingers or French bread

Serves 6

Miss J. S. Davidson · Wirral

Royal Stilton Tagliatelle

225g (8oz) tagliatelle verdi
100g (4oz) English butter
1 garlic clove, crushed
150ml (5 fl oz) fresh double cream
100g (4oz) Blue Stilton cheese, crumbled
1 tablespoon brandy
50g (2oz) pistachios

1 Cook the tagliatelle verdi according to the instructions on the packet. Drain

2 Gently heat the butter, add the garlic

3 Add the fresh cream and Stilton; heat gently until the cheese has melted. Stir in the brandy

4 Gently toss with the cooked tagliatelle and sprinkle with the pistachios. Serve immediately

Serves 4

Shauna Honig · London W2

Charnwood Smoked Pâté with Almonds

Stilton Mousse

100g (4oz) Blue Stilton cheese, grated
100g (4oz) Double Gloucester cheese, grated
300ml (10 fl oz) fresh double cream
25g (1oz) roasted almonds or cashew nuts, chopped
salt and freshly ground pepper
pinch of mustard powder
1 ½ teaspoons gelatine
2 egg whites

1 Mix both cheeses together. Lightly whip the fresh cream until softly stiff and stir into the cheese mixture with the nuts, seasoning and mustard

2 Place 2 tablespoons cold water in a small bowl and sprinkle in the gelatine. Stand the bowl over a saucepan of hot water and heat gently until dissolved

3 Fold the dissolved gelatine into the cheese mixture and leave in a cool place until half set. Stiffly whisk the egg whites and fold into the mousse, then pour into a 600ml (1 pint) soufflé dish or six individual dishes. Chill until set

4 Serve the mousse with a crisp green salad and melba toast

Serves 6

A. Coleman · Bordon

Avocado Dalesman

15g (½oz) English butter
1 tablespoon chopped onion
25g (1oz) mushrooms, chopped
1 ripe avocado
50g (2oz) Wensleydale cheese, grated
50g (2oz) cooked ham, diced
3–4 tablespoons fresh single cream
salt and freshly ground pepper

1 Melt the butter in a saucepan, add the onion and cook until soft but not browned. Stir in the mushrooms

2 Cut the avocado in half lengthways and remove stone. Carefully remove the flesh from the shells, reserving the shells. Dice the avocado and add to the mushroom mixture

3 Stir in the cheese and ham, then heat gently until the cheese melts

4 Stir in the cream and seasoning – do not make the mixture too runny. Place the avocado shells in serving dishes and spoon the mixture into them. Serve immediately

Serves 2

Mrs Lynn Mackenzie · Bradford

Stilton Avocado with Prawns

1 ripe avocado
100g (4oz) peeled prawns
4 tablespoons soured cream
50g (2oz) White Stilton cheese
pinch of salt
chopped chives

1 Halve the avocado, remove the stone and scoop out the flesh. Roughly chop the avocado flesh in a basin

2 Stir the prawns and soured cream into the avocado. Reserve a few prawns for garnish. Season to taste with salt

3 Crumble the cheese and mix half into avocado mixture. Spoon back into the avocado shells

4 Sprinkle the remaining cheese on top, then garnish with the chives and reserved prawns. Serve immediately

Serves 2

Mrs M. Catton · Bury St Edmunds

Crab and Cheese Boats

4 medium courgettes, washed and trimmed
25g (1oz) flour
25g (1oz) butter
300ml (½ pint) milk
salt and freshly ground pepper
100g (4oz) English Cheddar cheese, grated
100g (4oz) crab meat
2 small tomatoes, sliced

1 Cook the unpeeled courgettes in lightly salted simmering water until tender – about 10–15 minutes; drain and cut in half lengthways

2 Place the flour, butter and milk in a saucepan; heat, stirring continuously until the sauce thickens, boils and is smooth. Cook for 1 minute

3 Add 75g (3oz) of the cheese and seasoning to taste. Place the courgettes in a shallow ovenproof dish. Spread the crab meat over the cut sides. Coat the courgettes with the sauce and sprinkle over the remaining cheese

4 Place under a hot grill until golden and bubbling. Serve garnished with the tomato slices

Serves 4

Mrs J. Mervyn · Port St Mary

Gloucester Pears

99-g (3½-oz) can tuna
1 celery stalk, diced
1 large spring onion, chopped
150ml (¼ pint) thick mayonnaise
2 tablespoons wine vinegar or cider vinegar
freshly ground black pepper
1 small lettuce, washed
2 ripe dessert pears, halved and cored
100g (4oz) Double Gloucester cheese, diced
2 tomatoes, sliced

1 Flake the tuna into a bowl. Add the celery, onion, 4 tablespoons of the mayonnaise and 1 tablespoon of the vinegar, then season to taste with black pepper

2 Arrange the lettuce neatly on four individual plates

3 Cut a sliver from the rounded, skin side of each pear half to make sure they sit neatly with the cut side uppermost. Arrange them on the lettuce on the plates

4 Pile the tuna mixture into the hollow left by the core from each pear and surround with the diced cheese

5 Combine the remaining mayonnaise and vinegar and spoon over the stuffed pears. Garnish the plates with sliced tomato

6 Serve with thinly sliced wholemeal bread and butter

Serves 4

Miss A. M. Hedges · Oakham

Cheesy Mushrooms

4 large field mushrooms
50g (2oz) pâté
1 garlic clove, skinned and crushed
50g (2oz) fresh white breadcrumbs
100g (4oz) English Cheddar cheese, grated
salt and freshly ground pepper
25g (1oz) English butter
parsley sprigs

1 Place the mushrooms in buttered individual ovenproof dishes or on a buttered baking sheet. Mix the pâté, garlic and breadcrumbs together

2 Divide the pâté mixture between the mushrooms and sprinkle the cheese on the top. Add seasoning to taste. Dot the butter over and bake in the oven at 180°C (350°F), mark 4, for 20–25 minutes

3 Garnish with parsley sprigs and serve with hot French bread

Serves 4

Wendie Oliver · Bedford

Aubergine Erotica

2 small aubergines
50g (2oz) English butter
1 small onion, skinned and finely chopped
225g (8oz) minced beef
50g (2oz) mushrooms, chopped
427-g (15-oz) can tomatoes, drained
4 level teaspoons cornflour
150ml (¼ pint) milk
150ml (¼ pint) rosé wine
1 tablespoon fresh parsley, chopped
salt and freshly ground pepper
100g (4oz) English Cheddar cheese, grated
4 tablespoons dry white breadcrumbs
parsley sprigs
a few black olives

1 Wash the aubergines and prick them all over with a fork. Place on a baking tray and bake in the oven at 200°C (400°F), mark 6, for 20 minutes

2 Melt 25g (1oz) of the butter in a saucepan and fry the onion until soft but not browned. Add the minced beef and cook for 2 minutes before adding the mushrooms

3 Add the tomatoes to the beef mixture. Mix the cornflour to a smooth cream with a little of the milk, stir in the rest of the milk and the wine. Pour this mixture into the pan and cook, stirring continuously, until the mixtures boils and thickens. Add the chopped parsley and season to taste

4 Remove the aubergines from the oven and cut them in half lengthwise. Carefully scoop out all the flesh and chop it finely. Stir the chopped aubergine into the mince mixture and return it to the aubergine shells

5 Mix the cheese with the breadcrumbs and sprinkle over the aubergines. Dot with the remaining butter and return to the oven for a further 20 minutes

6 Garnish with fresh parsley sprigs and black olives

Serves 4

For a delicious supper dish, allow 1 whole aubergine per person and serve with hot French bread. Any leftover stuffing can be frozen when cold, then reheated and served on a bed of boiled rice

Mrs S. Amey · Bristol

When grating cheese, particularly the softer cheeses, it is difficult to remove the last pieces of cheese that stick to the grater.
To solve this, finish grating your cheese, then grate a chunk of bread a couple of times along the grater. This removes the last pieces of cheese and cleans the grater too.

Mrs M. Perkins · Bishops Stortford

Iced Pear Salad

Nutty Stuffed Cheddar Tomatoes

75g (3oz) unsalted peanuts, finely chopped
100g (4oz) English Cheddar cheese, grated
1 level teaspoon dried mixed herbs
½ level teaspoon dry mustard
salt and freshly ground pepper
2 slices wholemeal bread, with crusts removed
2 eggs
4 beef or very large tomatoes
watercress, washed and trimmed or parsley sprigs

1 Mix the peanuts, cheese, herbs, mustard and seasoning together. Reduce the bread to crumbs, then add to the cheese mixture and beat in the eggs

2 Cut and reserve the tops from the tomatoes. Scoop out most of the flesh and mix it into the cheese and nut filling mixture

3 Pile the filling into the tomatoes, replace the tops and place in buttered ovenproof dish. Bake in the oven at 190°C (375°F), mark 5, for 15–20 minutes, then transfer to a clean, warmed serving dish and garnish with watercress or parsley sprigs

4 Take care not to overcook the tomatoes or they will burst and look unattractive

Serves 4

Mrs M. A. Constable · Chester

Iced Pear Salad

3 tablespoons mayonnaise
100g (4oz) English Cheshire cheese, crumbled
1 red pepper, seeded and chopped
65ml (2½ fl oz) fresh double cream
2 large pears
4 lettuce leaves

1 Mix the mayonnaise, cheese, pepper and fresh cream and place in an ice tray or shallow container and place in the freezer

2 Stir mixture every 30 minutes until frozen (about 1 to 1½ hours)

3 Peel the pears, cut in half and remove the core. Place each half on a lettuce leaf and fill with a scoop of the iced cheese mixture. Serve immediately.

Serves 4

Mrs J. Jennings · Maidstone

Fresh Fruit and Cheese Cocktail

1 ripe advocado, halved and stoned
½ small honeydew melon
1 small, ripe, fresh pineapple, trimmed and cubed
100g (4oz) Blue Stilton cheese, cubed
150ml (¼ pint) mayonnaise
1 teaspoon apple cider vinegar
watercress, washed and trimmed
paprika

1 Peel the avocado halves and cut them into cubes

2 Scoop the seeds out of the melon and cube the flesh. Mix the avocado cubes with the melon and pineapple. Stir in the cheese, mayonnaise and vinegar. Chill lightly

3 Pile the fruit mixture on a serving platter and arrange the watercress around it. Sprinkle with paprika and serve with crisp melba toast

Serves 6–8

Margot Maddison · Chester

Crustacean Special

50g (2oz) English butter
1 medium onion, skinned and sliced
50g (2oz) mushrooms, sliced
1 tablespoon plain flour
150ml (¼ pint) milk
salt and freshly ground pepper
1 teaspoon Worcestershire sauce
1 tablespoon dry white wine or dry sherry
1 tablespoon wine vinegar
100g (4oz) English Cheddar cheese, grated
100g (4oz) crab meat

1 Melt the butter in a saucepan. Separate the onion slices into rings – reserve a few neat ones for garnish and add the remainder to the butter. Cook until soft but not browned

2 Stir the mushrooms into the butter and add the flour. Cook for a minute, then gradually add the milk and continue to cook, stirring continuously, until the sauce boils. Season to taste

3 Stir in the Worcestershire sauce, wine or sherry and vinegar. Add most of the cheese and stir until it melts

4 Stir the crab meat into the sauce. Divide between four scallop shells or individual ovenproof dishes and top with the remaining grated cheese

5 Brown under a hot grill and serve topped with the reserved onion rings

Serves 4

Margaret Harris · Norwich

Cheesy Prawns

100g (4oz) peeled prawns
salt and freshly ground pepper
150ml (5 fl oz) fresh double cream
8 tablespoons browned breadcrumbs
100g (4oz) English Cheddar cheese, grated
25g (1oz) English butter
chopped parsley

1 Butter four individual ovenproof dishes and divide the prawns between them. Season and divide the fresh cream between the dishes

2 Sprinkle the breadcrumbs over and then top with the grated cheese. Dot with butter. Bake in the oven at 200°C (400°F), mark 6, for 15 minutes or until browned and bubbling hot

3 Serve immediately, sprinkled with chopped parsley

Serves 4

Mrs P. Smith · Kenilworth

Cheese and Smoked Chicken Ramekins

25g (1oz) plain flour
25g (1oz) English butter
568ml (1 pint) milk
75g (3oz) English Cheddar cheese, grated
75g (3oz) Lancashire cheese, grated
salt and freshly ground pepper
350g (12oz) smoked chicken, cut into chunks
paprika

1 Place the flour, butter and milk in a saucepan; heat, stirring continuously until the sauce thickens, boils and is smooth. Cook for 1 minute

2 Stir the Cheddar and 50g (2oz) of the Lancashire cheese into the sauce. Add seasoning to taste

3 Divide the chicken between six individual ovenproof dishes and pour the sauce over. Top with the remaining Lancashire cheese and bake in the oven at 200°C (400°F), mark 6, for about 20 minutes, until golden brown and bubbling hot

4 Sprinkle a little paprika over each serving and serve immediately with hot French bread

Serves 6

C. Astbury · Weedon

Kohlrabi Cheese Ramekins

4 medium kohlrabi (about the size of tennis balls)
350g (12oz) smoked haddock fillet, skinned and flaked
25g (1oz) nibbed mixed nuts
50g (2oz) fresh white breadcrumbs
salt and freshly ground pepper
75g (3oz) English Cheddar cheese, finely grated
chopped parsley

1 Peel and wash the kohlrabi, then slice and cut them into cubes

2 Boil the kohlrabi in lightly salted water for 20–25 minutes. Drain and reduce to a fine purée in a liquidiser

3 Stir the haddock, nuts and breadcrumbs into the vegetable purée, add seasoning to taste and mix well. Spoon the mixture into individual ramekins or ovenproof dishes and spread evenly, leaving a 1cm (½ inch) space at the top of the dish

4 Sprinkle a generous topping of grated cheese over each ramekin. Bake in the oven at 180°C (350°F), mark 4, for 15 minutes, then place the ramekins under a hot grill for 3 minutes to brown the cheese. Serve at once, garnished with chopped parsley. Alternatively leeks could be used instead of kohlrabi

Serves 4

Mr Ian D. Hendry · By Banchory

Staffords Cheese and Seafood Special

350g (12oz) cod
½ onion, finely chopped
40g (1½oz) English butter
15g (½oz) cornflour
200ml (7 fl oz) milk
50g (2oz) ground almonds
½ level teaspoon ground mace
parsley sprig, finely chopped
100g (4oz) peeled prawns
salt and pepper
50g (2oz) Leicester cheese, grated
2 tablespoons breadcrumbs
lemon slices
4 unshelled prawns

1 Wash fish, remove skin and bones, cut into small cubes

2 Gently fry onion in 25g (1oz) butter, add cornflour and cook over a low heat, stirring continuously, for 2 minutes

3 Gradually blend in milk; heat, stirring continuously until the sauce thickens, boils and is smooth

4 Add the fish, ground almonds, mace, parsley, prawns and seasoning to taste. Simmer for 10 minutes

5 Turn into 4 scallop shells. Mix cheese and breadcrumbs together and sprinkle on top. Dot with remaining butter

6 Grill until golden brown. Serve immediately with lemon slices and prawns

Serves 4

Mrs J. V. Huxley · Runcorn

Staffords Cheese and Seafood Special

Celery with Stilton and Port Sauce

6 celery sticks, taken from the centre of the head
25g (1oz) English butter
3 tablespoons plain flour
300ml (½ pint) milk
salt and freshly ground pepper
100g (4oz) White Stilton cheese
3 tablespoons port

1 Clean the celery and cut each stick into 2·5cm (1 inch) lengths

2 Boil the pieces of celery in water until tender – about 10 minutes

3 Melt the butter in a saucepan and stir in the flour. Cook over low heat for 2 minutes. Gradually stir in the milk, bring to the boil, stirring continuously, and cook for 1 minute. Add seasoning to taste

4 Add the cheese and stir until melted, then remove the pan from the heat and stir in the port

5 Drain the celery and place in an ovenproof dish. Pour over the Stilton sauce and brown under a hot grill

6 Serve immediately with fresh crusty bread

Serves 6

Linda Drake · London SE15

Cheddar Smokies

450g (1lb) smoked haddock fillets, skinned
1 bay leaf
50g (2oz) English butter
50g (2oz) plain flour
175g (6oz) English Cheddar cheese, grated
freshly ground black pepper
1 glass dry white wine

1 Poach the haddock in 900ml (1½ pints) water with the bay leaf for about 15 minutes until cooked. Cool slightly and then remove from liquor and keep to one side. Reserve 600ml (1 pint) of the fish liquor and discard bayleaf

2 Melt the butter in a saucepan, stir in the flour to make a roux. Cook for 1 to 2 minutes, stirring continuously. Gradually add the reserved fish liquor, bring to the boil, stirring all the time and simmer for 15 minutes

3 Stir 100g (4oz) of the cheese, black pepper and wine into the sauce

4 Flake the haddock and add to the sauce. Divide between 8 ramekin dishes and sprinkle remaining cheese on top. Place under a hot grill until golden brown

Serves 8

Mrs Zena M. Probyn · St Martin

Leek and White Stilton Soup

3 medium leeks, trimmed, washed and chopped
25g (1oz) English butter
25g (1oz) plain flour
568ml (1 pint) milk
1 chicken stock cube
150ml (¼ pint) boiling water
100g (4oz) White Stilton cheese, finely grated
fresh single cream
4–6 tablespoons fresh croûtons
1 tablespoon chopped chives (optional)

1 Cook leeks in a little water until tender

2 Melt the butter in a large saucepan, add the leeks and cook, stirring, over low heat for 5 minutes. Add the flour and stir over low heat for a few minutes

3 Gradually add the milk, stirring continuously over low heat. If the mixture shows any signs of forming lumps, remove the pan from the heat and beat thoroughly before adding more liquid

4 Dissolve the stock cube in the boiling water and add to the soup. Sieve or liquidise until smooth

5 Return the soup to the pan and bring to the boil. Remove from the heat and add the grated cheese slowly, stirring continuously until melted

6 Serve immediately, topped with a little fresh cream and garnished with croûtons — small cubes of bread fried in butter — or chives.

Serves 4

E. M. Beaumont · Middlesbrough

Cheese and Onion Soup

1 large onion, chopped
25g (1oz) English butter
25g (1oz) flour
1 level teaspoon mustard powder
568ml (1 pint) milk
150ml (¼ pint) chicken stock
salt and pepper
100g (4oz) Lancashire cheese, crumbled
paprika

1 Fry onion in butter until soft. Add the flour and mustard and cook slowly for 2 minutes. Blend in milk and stock and bring to the boil, stirring continuously

2 Season to taste and leave to simmer gently for 15 minutes

3 Remove from the heat and add the cheese, stir until melted. Ladle into warm soup bowls and serve sprinkled with paprika

Serves 4

Cheese and Vegetable Soup

4 carrots, diced
2 onions, finely chopped
2 sticks of celery, finely chopped
450ml (¾ pint) water
1 teaspoon salt
25g (1oz) flour
300ml (½ pint) milk
100g (4oz) English Cheddar cheese, finely grated
25g (1oz) English butter
salt and pepper

1 Place vegetables, water and salt in a saucepan, and cook for 20–30 minutes

2 Mix flour to a smooth paste with milk. Add to the saucepan, stirring continuously, and bring the soup to the boil. Simmer for 5 minutes

3 Remove from the heat and add cheese and the butter. Stir until both have melted

4 Season to taste, serve in warmed soup bowls

Serves 4

Stilton Soup

25 (1oz) English butter
1 onion, skinned and finely chopped
5 celery sticks, finely chopped
25g (1oz) plain flour
75ml (2 ½ fl oz) dry white wine
600ml (1 pint) chicken stock
150ml (¼ pint) milk
100g (4oz) Blue Stilton cheese, crumbled
salt and freshly ground pepper
75ml (2 ½ fl oz) fresh double cream

1 Melt the butter in a saucepan. Add the onion and celery and cook until soft but not browned — about 5 minutes

2 Add the flour and cook for a further minute, then move the pan from the heat

3 Stir in the wine and stock and return to the heat. Bring to the boil, stirring continuously until the soup thickens, then simmer over low heat for 30 minutes

4 Cool slightly and liquidise or press the soup through a sieve. Return to the rinsed-out pan

5 Add the milk and heat gently. Stir in the Stilton until melted, seasoning and the fresh cream. Do not let the soup boil at this stage, or it will curdle. Serve hot or chilled

Serves 4–6

Margaret Simpson · Reigate

Top: Cheese and Vegetable Soup. Left to right: Stilton Soup, Gloucestershire Chowder, Cheese and Crab Soup

Gloucestershire Chowder

2 medium potatoes, peeled and diced
600ml (1 pint) water
salt and freshly ground pepper
1 bay leaf
1 level teaspoon dried sage
1 level teaspoon ground cumin (optional)
1 large onion, skinned and chopped
25g (1oz) English butter
100g (4oz) sweet corn
50g (2oz) frozen peas
150ml (5 fl oz) fresh single cream
100g (4oz) Double Gloucester cheese, grated
½ level teaspoon grated nutmeg

1 Put the potatoes, water and seasoning in a saucepan with the bay leaf, sage and cumin, bring to the boil and simmer for about 15 minutes. Remove the bay leaf

2 Sauté the onion in the butter until soft but not browned, then add to the boiled potatoes and their cooking liquid. Add the corn and peas, then simmer for 5 minutes. Add a little extra water if the soup is too thick

3 Stir in the fresh cream, cheese and nutmeg and stir over very low heat until the cheese has melted. Serve immediately

Serves 4

Mrs C. Scott · Oxfordshire

Cheese and Crab Soup

50g (2oz) English butter
1 small onion, skinned and finely chopped
50g (2oz) plain flour
1 litre (1¾ pints) chicken stock
150g (5oz) white crab meat
100g (4oz) Lancashire cheese, crumbled
salt and freshly ground pepper
chopped chives

1 Melt the butter in a saucepan. Add the onion, then cook gently until soft but not browned. Add the flour, stirring constantly, and pour in the stock, still stirring

2 Bring to the boil, then simmer for 5 minutes. Put the crab meat and crumbled cheese into a liquidiser. Add enough soup to moisten the ingredients and reduce them to a smooth purée

3 Return the soup to the pan, then simmer gently for 5 minutes. Add seasoning to taste and serve garnished with chopped chives

Serves 4–6

Mrs M. Street · Paignton

To add zest to celery soup; to each bowl add 1 tablespoon lightly whipped fresh double cream, then sprinkle with crumbled Blue Stilton cheese

Mrs E. Browning · Glasgow

Lunch and Supper Dishes

Welsh rarebit is everyone's favourite. It is speedy to prepare and nourishing too, and the variations of cheese on toast are endless. Pies and burgers, fish and pasta all fall within the family favourites and not to be overlooked, the basic pancake and omelette which lend themselves to so many fillings with cheese.

English Cheese Roll

2 medium onions, skinned and finely chopped
½ red pepper, seeded and chopped
25g (1oz) English butter
100g (4oz) fresh white breadcrumbs
3 tablespoons fresh single cream
1 level teaspoon dried oregano
salt and freshly ground black pepper
350g (12oz) minced beef
100g (4oz) minced bacon
2 tablespoons tomato purée
1 egg, beaten
2 tomatoes, thinly sliced
150g (5oz) English Cheddar cheese, grated
4 tablespoons spicy tomato ketchup
1 tablespoon soft brown sugar
pinch of dry mustard
fried onion rings

1 Sauté onion and pepper in butter until soft but not browned and drain well

2 Mix breadcrumbs, fresh cream, oregano, seasoning, beef, bacon, 1 tablespoon tomato purée, egg and half of the sautéed mixture and combine thoroughly

3 Place the mixture on a sheet of greaseproof paper placed on a damp teatowel. Cover with another sheet of greaseproof paper and shape into an oblong 30·5 × 20·5cm (12 × 8 inches). Remove the top layer of paper

4 Mix the remaining onion and peppers with 1 tablespoon tomato purée and spread over two-thirds of the meat mixture to within 2·5cm (1 inch) of the outer edges

5 Arrange tomatoes on top and sprinkle with cheese, leaving one-third of meat uncovered

6 Starting from the filled end, carefully roll up lengthways like a Swiss roll. Wrap in a piece of foil and lift on to a baking sheet

7 Bake 180°C (350°F), mark 4, for 35 minutes

8 Mix tomato ketchup, sugar and mustard together. Open foil and brush mixture all over the meat roll. Return to the oven, uncovered, for a further 20 minutes until the top is slightly brown. Serve garnished with onion rings

Serves 4–6

Carol Ann Bowers · Newton le Willows

Golden Cheddar Surprise

1 onion, skinned and coarsley chopped
2 tablespoons vegetable oil
450g (1lb) cooked hock bacon joint, cubed
juice of 2 oranges, or 4 tablespoons concentrated orange
    juice
1 level teaspoon cornflour
salt and pepper
100g (4oz) English butter
225g (8oz) wholemeal flour
¼ level teaspoon dried mixed herbs
100g (4oz) English Cheddar cheese, sliced thinly

1 Fry onion in oil until soft but not browned. Divide onion and bacon between 4 individual ovenproof dishes or soup bowls

2 Make orange juice up to 300ml (½ pint) with water. Blend cornflour with a little of the juice and then add to the remaining juice and season to taste. Pour into the dishes

3 Rub butter into the flour until the mixture resembles fine breadcrumbs. Add mixed herbs. Sprinkle one-quarter of this crumble over the bacon and orange in each bowl

4 Bake 180°C (350°F); mark 4, for 30 minutes

5 Place overlapping slices of cheese to form a complete seal over the crumble in each bowl

6 Place under a hot grill for a few minutes. Serve immediately

Serves 4

Mrs T. Griffiths · Dunblane

English Cheese Roll

Two Cheese Bake

450g (1lb) minced beef
25g (1oz) English butter
1 tablespoon vegetable oil
175ml (6 fl oz) tomato juice
175g (6oz) cottage cheese
175ml (6 fl oz) soured cream
175g (6oz) onions, skinned and chopped
3 tablespoons chopped parsley
225g (8oz) noodles, cooked and drained
225g (8oz) English Cheddar cheese, grated

1 Fry the beef in butter and oil for 10 minutes

2 Add tomato juice and simmer for 5 minutes

3 Mix cottage cheese, soured cream, onions and parsley with the noodles

4 Arrange alternate layers of meat and noodles in a buttered ovenproof dish. Sprinkle cheese on top

5 Bake 180°C (350°F), mark 4, for 20 to 25 minutes

Serves 4

Barbara Joan Massey · Colchester

Lancashire Gammon

25g (1oz) English butter
4 gammon steaks
25g (1oz) plain flour
300ml (½ pint) milk
100g (4oz) Lancashire cheese, crumbled
1½ tablespoons fresh single cream
salt and pepper
2 eggs, hard-boiled and sliced
parsley sprigs

1 Melt butter in a large frying pan and fry gammon steaks on both sides. Transfer to a shallow ovenproof dish

2 Add flour and milk to the butter left in the pan. Heat, stirring continuously until the sauce thickens and is smooth. Cook for 1 minute. Remove from heat and stir in, off the heat, 75g (3oz) of the cheese, fresh cream, salt and pepper

3 Arrange slices of hard-boiled egg on top of gammon and coat with cheese sauce; sprinkle the remaining cheese over the top

4 Bake 200°C (400°F), mark 6, for 15 minutes. Garnish with parsley and serve with buttered noodles and peas

Serves 4

Rose Kingsbury · Stoke on Trent

Pepper Mac

4 large green peppers, with tops removed and seeded
50g (2oz) English butter
1 medium onion, skinned and chopped
100g (4oz) cooked ham, chopped
300ml (½ pint) milk
25g (1oz) plain flour
salt and freshly ground pepper
175g (6oz) English Cheshire cheese, grated
100g (4oz) cooked macaroni
3 tablespoons fresh breadcrumbs

1 Blanch the peppers in boiling water for 5 minutes. Drain on absorbent kitchen paper

2 Melt half the butter in a frying pan, add the onion and cook until soft but not browned. Stir in the ham and cook for 2 minutes. Set aside

3 Place the remaining butter, milk and flour in a saucepan; heat, stirring continuously until the sauce thickens, boils and is smooth. Cook for 1 minute. Add seasoning to taste

4 Stir in half the cheese, onion mixture and macaroni, off the heat, and stir until the cheese melts. Spoon this filling into the peppers and stand them in an ovenproof dish

5 Mix the remaining cheese with the breadcrumbs and sprinkle over the peppers

6 Bake in the oven at 190°C (375°F), mark 5, for 30 minutes, or until golden brown on top. Serve immediately

Serves 4

Ann Bramwell · Woodhouse

Savoury Beetroot

2 large beetroot, cooked and skinned
175g (6oz) Leicester cheese, grated
300ml (½ pint) white sauce (page 116)
2 level teaspoons made mustard
225g (8oz) mixed diced vegetables, cooked and drained
3 tablespoons fresh brown breadcrumbs
25g (1oz) English butter

1 Cut each beetroot into 4 slices, and place in an ovenproof dish

2 Stir 100g (4oz) of the cheese into the sauce, off the heat, with the mustard

3 Add the hot vegetables and pile the mixture on to the beetroot slices

4 Top with the breadcrumbs and remaining cheese, dot with butter and grill until golden

Serves 4

Mrs Margaret Emmerson · Grimsby

Left: Pepper Mac. Right: Cheddar Horseshoes

Pork Derby

2 loin of pork chops
freshly ground black pepper
3 tablespoons lemon juice
3 tablespoons olive oil
1 bay leaf, crumbled
¼ level teaspoon dried thyme
100g (4oz) Sage Derby cheese, sliced

1 With a sharp knife carefully slice the chops horizontally from the outer edge of fat, towards the small bone to make a 'pocket'

2 Use your hands to rub the surface of the meat with freshly ground black pepper

3 Make a marinade with the lemon juice, oil and herbs, mixing well together

4 Place the pork in the marinade and coat evenly. Cover and leave in the refrigerator for 2–3 hours, turning occasionally

5 Drain the meat and reserve marinade. Insert slices of cheese into the 'pocket' of each chop

6 Place under a hot grill until cooked, turning occasionally and basting with reserved marinade. Serve with new boiled potatoes and a crisp green salad

Serves 2

S. W. A. Lambert · Alcester

Cheddar Horseshoes

275g (10oz) pork fillet
100g (4oz) English Cheddar cheese
dried rosemary, crushed
salt and freshly ground black pepper
8 miniature cocktail gherkins, halved lengthways
100g (4oz) red pepper, seeded and cut into 16 squares
juice of ½ lemon
175g (6oz) rice, cooked

1 Place pork between greaseproof paper and beat until thin with a rolling pin. Cut into 16 slices

2 Slice cheese thinly into 16 slices and place a piece of cheese on each slice of pork, sprinkle with rosemary and seasoning and lay ½ gherkin on each

3 Fold meat in half to enclose the topping ingredients. Thread carefully on to four kebab or kitchen skewers, making sure skewers go through meat, cheese, gherkins and meat again to make a horseshoe shape. Place a piece of red pepper in between each horseshoe

4 Place under a hot grill for 5 minutes then pour over the lemon juice and grill for a further 5 minutes. Serve on a bed of rice

Serves 4

Mrs R. G. Rotella · Hove

Country-style Turkey Pie

1 medium onion, skinned and chopped
4 rashers streaky bacon, rinded and chopped
50g (2oz) mushrooms, peeled and chopped
15g (½oz) English butter
300ml (½ pint) white sauce (page 116)
2 tablespoons dry sherry
½ teaspoon Worcestershire sauce
1 tablespoon turkey stock
450g (1lb) cold cooked turkey (or chicken), diced
¼ level teaspoon dried mixed herbs
100g (4oz) shortcrust pastry made with 100g (4oz) plain
　flour (page 116)
75g (3oz) mature English Cheddar cheese, finely grated

1 Sauté onion, bacon and mushrooms in butter

2 Stir into the white sauce the sherry, Worcestershire
sauce and turkey stock

3 Stir in the turkey, cooked onion, bacon, mushroom
and mixed herbs. Place in a 1 litre (1½ pint) pie dish

4 Make up half-quantity shortcrust pastry (page 116).
Knead lightly and roll out on a lightly floured work top
and cover the pie dish. Decorate with pastry leaves and
sprinkle with cheese

5 Bake 200°C (400°F), mark 6, for 30 minutes

Serves 4

G. E. Crawford · Pinner

Ploughman's Pork Chops

4 boneless pork chops
1 tablespoon vegetable oil
25g (1oz) English butter
salt and freshly ground pepper
pinch of celery salt
150ml (¼ pint) chicken stock
2 cooking apples, peeled, cored and finely chopped
1 tablespoon sweet sherry
2 tablespoons caster sugar
1 tablespoon sultanas
1 level teaspoon fresh chopped sage
100g (4oz) English Cheddar cheese, grated
parsley sprigs

1 Fry chops in oil and butter for about 5 minutes each
side. Season to taste, add celery salt and stock. Cover
and simmer for 30 minutes

2 Place the apples in a saucepan, add sherry, sugar,
sultanas and sage. Cook 1–2 minutes until tender.
Remove from the heat

3 Add cheese and stir well

4 Spoon a little of the apple mixture on top of each
chop. Cover and simmer for a further 5 minutes until the
cheese just begins to melt. Serve remaining mixture
separately. Garnish with parsley

Serves 4

Mrs A. Elliker · Leeds

Left: Country-style Turkey Pie. Centre: Ploughman's Pork Chops

Moussaka

75g (3oz) English butter
2 tablespoons oil
1 onion, peeled and chopped
450g (1lb) minced beef or lamb
salt and pepper
1 tablespoon tomato purée
150ml (¼ pint) stock or water
3 aubergines, sliced thinly
25g (1oz) flour
300ml (½ pint) milk
100g (4oz) English Cheddar cheese, grated
1 egg, beaten

1 Heat 25g (1oz) butter and 1 tablespoon oil and fry the onion for 5 minutes. Add the minced meat and fry until brown

2 Stir in salt and pepper, tomato purée and stock. Bring to the boil, cover the pan and simmer for 30 minutes or until the meat is cooked

3 Meanwhile place aubergine slices on a plate and sprinkle generously with salt. Leave for 30 minutes, drain, rinse and dry. Fry in remaining oil and 25g (1oz) butter until golden. Drain

4 Arrange alternate layers of aubergine and meat in large buttered ovenproof dish, starting and finishing with aubergines

5 Place remaining butter, flour and milk into a saucepan. Heat, stirring continuously until the mixture thickens, boils and is smooth. Cook for 1 minute. Remove from the heat and add 75g (3oz) of the cheese, stir until melted and season to taste. Allow sauce to cool a little and beat in the egg

6 Pour the sauce over the moussaka and sprinkle reserved cheese on top. Bake 180°C (350°F), mark 4, for 35 minutes or until brown and bubbling

Serves 4

Stuffed Courgettes with Cheese and Yogurt Sauce

4–6 courgettes, trimmed
1 small onion, skinned and chopped
90g (3½oz) English butter
175g (6oz) fresh wholemeal breadcrumbs
sea salt and freshly ground black pepper
1 level tablespoon dried dill (optional)
2 tablespoons plain flour
450ml (¾ pint) milk
75g (3oz) mature English Farmhouse Cheddar cheese, grated
100g (4oz) natural yogurt
1 egg, separated

1 Cook whole courgettes in boiling salted water for 8 to 10 minutes. Drain and cool

2 Cut in half lengthways and hollow out flesh from the centres and chop

3 Fry onion in 50g (2oz) of the butter until soft, add chopped courgette flesh and cook for 2 minutes

4 Add breadcrumbs and cook for further 1 to 2 minutes, stirring well. Remove from heat, add seasoning to taste and dill and allow to cool

5 Fill courgette shells with the stuffing and place in buttered ovenproof dish

6 Place the flour, remaining butter and milk in a saucepan; heat, stirring continuously until the sauce thickens, boils and is smooth. Cook for 1 minute. Remove from the heat, add cheese and stir off the heat until it has melted. Add more seasoning to taste, yogurt and egg yolk, stirring until well mixed

7 Whisk egg white until it stands in stiff peaks. Fold into sauce and spoon over courgettes

8 Bake 190°C (375°F), mark 5, for 12 to 15 minutes. Serve with a salad

Serves 4

Christine Jackson · Nottingham

For a savoury topping grate leftover or dry cheese and mix with an equal amount of sage and onion stuffing
Store in an airtight container. Use to sprinkle over savoury dishes. Place under a medium grill to give a quick crunchy topping

E. E. Rushton · Anglesey

Spiced Fish

450g (1lb) cod fillet, skinned and cut into 5cm (2 inch)
   strips
2 level teaspoons tumeric
3 tablespoons vegetable oil
2 medium onions, skinned and chopped
5cm (2 inch) piece of cinnamon stick
½ level teaspoon hot chilli powder
2 sticks of celery, chopped
2 carrots, peeled and chopped
142g (5oz) natural yogurt
50g (2oz) mixed nuts, chopped
salt and pepper
100g (4oz) English Cheddar cheese, grated
450g (1lb) potatoes, cooked and creamed

1 Coat the fish in tumeric and fry quickly in oil for 5
minutes, turning once. Remove from pan

2 Fry the onions and cinnamon stick in the oil until
golden brown

3 Add chilli powder, celery, carrot and fry for 10
minutes. Remove from heat

4 Stir in the yogurt, a tablespoon at a time. Add 4
tablespoons of water, nuts, seasoning to taste. Add fish
and simmer for 10 minutes until cooked

5 Transfer to an ovenproof casserole and sprinkle with
50g (2oz) cheese

6 Add remaining cheese to potatoes and pipe around the
edge of the dish. Grill until golden brown

Serves 4

Nicola Sparkes · Norwich

Haddock with Banana and Almonds

2 bananas, cut in half lengthways
65g (2½oz) English butter
450g (1lb) haddock
salt and pepper
100g (4oz) streaky bacon rashers, rinded
2 onions, skinned and sliced
40g (1½oz) flour
300ml (½ pint) milk
150g (5oz) English Cheddar cheese, grated
2 tablespoons sherry
25g (1oz) flaked almonds

1 Fry the bananas quickly in 25g (1oz) butter until golden
brown

2 Poach the fish in salted water for 10 minutes or until
tender. Reserve 150ml (¼ pint) of the liquor for stock.
Flake fish, discarding any skin and bones

3 Layer the fish and bananas alternately in a buttered
1·1 litre (2 pint) ovenproof dish, seasoning to taste as
you go

4 Fry the bacon slices in their own fat, remove from the
pan and fry the onions until soft. Place bacon and
onions over the fish and bananas

5 Place remaining butter, flour, milk and fish liquor into a
saucepan. Heat, stirring continuously until the sauce
thickens, boils and is smooth. Stir in 100g (4oz) cheese
and sherry, off the heat, and pour sauce over the fish.
Sprinkle with remaining cheese and almonds

6 Bake 200°C (400°F), mark 6, for 15−20 minutes or until
the topping is golden brown

Serves 4

Left: Spiced Fish. Right: Haddock with Banana and Almonds

'Lanky' Liver

225g (8oz) lamb's liver, washed, trimmed, cubed
1 tablespoon plain flour
1 tablespoon vegetable oil
1 large onion, skinned and finely chopped
4 fresh sage leaves, chopped
300ml (½ pint) stock
salt and freshly ground black pepper
75g (3oz) fresh white breadcrumbs
75g (3oz) Lancashire cheese, crumbled

1 Toss liver in flour and fry in oil until the juices begin to run

2 Add the onion and sage and fry until the onion is soft but not brown

3 Stir in the stock and seasoning to taste and place in a casserole

4 Cover with breadcrumbs and cheese

5 Bake 190°C (375°F), mark 5, for 15 minutes until golden brown. Serve immediately

Serves 4

Mrs Dorothy Smith · Oswaldtwistle

Cheese and Noodle Hotpot

225g (8oz) flat noodles
1 onion, chopped
25g (1oz) English butter
25g (1oz) flour
300ml (½ pint) milk
2 tablespoons tomato purée
50g (2oz) hazelnuts, chopped
225g (8oz) Lancashire cheese, crumbled
salt and pepper
1 tomato, sliced
parsley

1 Cook the noodles in boiling salted water until tender. Drain

2 Gently fry the onion in butter until golden. Add the flour and cook for 2 minutes. Gradually blend in the milk, heat, stirring continuously until the sauce thickens, boils and is smooth. Cook for 1 minute

3 Add the noodles, purée, hazelnuts and 175g (6oz) cheese, off the heat. Mix thoroughly and season to taste

4 Pour into a 1·1 litre (2 pint) buttered fireproof dish and sprinkle with remaining cheese

5 Bake 190°C (375°F), mark 5, for 20 and 25 minutes or until top is golden

6 Serve garnished with tomato slices and parsley

Serves 4

Cheesy Bacon Crumble

vegetable oil for shallow frying
1 cooking apple, peeled, cored and chopped
1 small onion, skinned and chopped
175g (6oz) streaky bacon, rinded and chopped
salt and freshly ground pepper
75g (3oz) English Cheddar cheese
50g (2oz) fresh white breadcrumbs
2 tablespoons chopped fresh parsley or chives (optional)

1 Heat the oil in a frying pan, add the apple, onion and bacon and cook until very soft. Add seasoning to taste, then transfer the mixture to an ovenproof dish

2 Mix the cheese with the breadcrumbs and herbs (if used), then sprinkle over the top of the bacon mixture in an even layer

3 Place under a hot grill until golden brown and serve immediately

Serves 2–4

Mrs R. Semplis · Slough

Cheesy Fish Surprise

370-g (13-oz) packet frozen puff pastry, thawed
175–225g (6–8oz) smoked mackerel, flaked
3 tomatoes, skinned and chopped
½ green pepper, seeded and chopped
225g (8oz) English Cheddar cheese, grated
pinch of dried mixed herbs
pinch of cayenne
salt and pepper
1 teaspoon tomato purée
beaten egg

1 Roll pastry on a lightly floured work top, to an oblong 35 × 56cm (14 × 22 inches). Cut in half and place 1 half on a dampened baking sheet

2 Mix the fish with the tomatoes, pepper, cheese, mixed herbs and seasonings to taste and bind with tomato purée

3 Spread over the pastry to within 2·5cm (1 inch) of the edges

4 Slit the remaining piece of pastry to within 2·5cm (1 inch) of the edges at 2·5cm (1 inch) intervals. Place on top of mixture. Seal the edges and flute to decorate. Brush with beaten egg

5 Bake 200°C (425°F), mark 7, for 30 minutes

Serves 4

Mrs Jeanette Albinson · Poole

Pancakes

100g (4oz) flour
salt
1 egg
300ml (½ pint) milk
1 tablespoon melted butter
1 tablespoon oil

1 Sift the flour and salt into a mixing bowl. Make a well in the centre and put in the egg

2 Gradually add half the milk, beating in the flour vigorously with a wooden spoon until a thick creamy batter is formed. Pour in the remaining milk and melted butter. Beat until quite smooth

3 To season the pan, heat 1 tablespoon oil in a frying pan. Sprinkle with salt. Wipe out with absorbent kitchen paper

4 Heat a little oil in the seasoned pan and when very hot pour in a little of the batter. Tip the pan quickly so the batter runs over the bottom of the pan

5 Cook over high heat until the underneath is golden brown, then turn the pancake. Cook the other side until golden brown

6 Repeat for 8 pancakes

Serves 4

Variations

Country Pancakes

Stuff pancakes with cooked mushrooms and tomatoes. Cover with cheese sauce (refer page 116). Sprinkle with grated English Cheddar cheese and brown under a hot grill

Ham and Cheese Pancakes

Lightly fry 225g (8oz) chopped ham in English butter, add 175g (6oz) grated English Cheddar cheese, pinch of dried mixed herbs and seasoning. Use to fill the pancakes. Warm under the grill. Serve immediately garnished with tomato

Chicken and Tarragon Pancakes

Make up cheese sauce (refer page 116), add chopped cooked chicken, lightly fried mushrooms and onions and ½ level teaspoon dried tarragon. Use to fill the pancakes. Pour any remaining sauce over the top and grill, topped with grated English cheese

Cow and Calf Pancakes

1 large onion, skinned and finely chopped
15g (½oz) English butter
225g (8oz) minced beef
1–2 sticks of celery, chopped
1–2 garlic cloves, skinned and crushed
salt and freshly ground black pepper
100g (4oz) Blue Stilton cheese, rinded
a little fresh cream
8 pancakes using 300ml (½ pint) pancake batter (see Pancakes)

1 Fry onion in butter until soft, but not browned. Add minced beef, celery and garlic and fry until cooked. Add seasoning to taste

2 Mash the cheese with a little fresh cream until a soft, smooth consistency is obtained. Keep filling hot

3 Make up pancakes according to pancake recipe instructions. Fill each pancake with a little of the meat mixture and roll up. Place a spoonful of cheese mixture on top of each pancake. Serve with baked tomatoes

Serves 4

Violetta Hill · London SE3

Left to right: Cow and Calf Pancakes, Bacon and Mushroom Omelette, Pizza

Cheese Omelette

3 eggs
4 teaspoons cold water
salt and pepper
25g (1oz) English butter
50g (2oz) English Cheddar cheese, grated

1 Beat eggs and water lightly together. Add salt and pepper

2 Melt the butter in an omelette pan until very hot

3 Pour in the beaten eggs

4 After 5 seconds move the edges of the setting omelette to the centre of the pan with a knife. At the same time tilt the pan in all directions so that the uncooked egg flows to the edges

5 Cook for a further ½–1 minute until the underneath is set and the top slightly moist

6 Sprinkle with the grated cheese, and allow the cheese to melt a little

7 Remove the pan from the heat. Fold omelette in half and slide it on to a warm serving plate. Serve immediately

Serves 2

Variations

Bacon and Mushroom Omelette

Gently fry, in a little English butter, finely chopped lean bacon, mushrooms and onions. Add to the beaten eggs

Apple and Wensleydale Omelette

Replace the English Cheddar with chopped apple and Wensleydale cheese

Pizza

100g (4oz) cottage cheese
115g (4½oz) English butter
100g (4oz) wholemeal flour
1 onion, skinned and chopped
1 garlic clove, skinned and crushed
215-g (7½-oz) can tomatoes
1 tablespoon tomato purée
½ level teaspoon dried oregano
½ level teaspoon dried basil
salt and pepper
150g (5oz) English Cheddar cheese, grated
50-g (1¾-oz) can anchovies, drained

1 Mix cottage cheese and 100g (4oz) butter together and gradually work in the flour and bind to make a cheese pastry. Wrap in greaseproof paper and chill

2 Sauté onion and garlic in remaining butter until soft but not browned

3 Add tomatoes, tomato purée, herbs and seasoning to taste. Cook until most of the liquid has evaporated. Allow to cool

4 Roll out the chilled pastry on a lightly floured work top, into a 20cm (8 inch) round and pinch the edge so that it is slightly raised. Place on a baking sheet

5 Spread tomato mixture over the pastry and sprinkle with the grated cheese

6 Arrange anchovies on top in a lattice design

7 Bake 220°C (425°F), mark 7, for 15 minutes, then reduce temperature to 190°C (375°F), mark 5, for 20 to 25 minutes. Serve hot or cold

Serves 4–6

Anne Whitehead · Newcastle-upon-Tyne

Welsh Rarebit

4 pieces of French bread sliced in half
25g (1oz) English butter, softened
1 level teaspoon made mustard
salt
cayenne
¼ teaspoon Worcestershire sauce
175g (6oz) Lancashire cheese, crumbled, or English
   Cheddar cheese, grated
2 tablespoons milk
slices of stuffed olives

1 Toast bread on crusty side only

2 Cream butter well and stir in mustard, salt, cayenne, Worcestershire sauce, cheese and milk

3 Spread equal amounts thickly over untoasted sides of bread

4 Brown under hot grill and top with stuffed olives

Serves 4

Variations

Bacon Rarebit

Top Welsh Rarebit with 2 slices of grilled or fried bacon

Tomato Rarebit

Top Welsh Rarebit with 2 or 3 grilled or fried tomato slices on top

---

To give a sharp piquant flavour to Welsh rarebit, add 1 tablespoon unsweetened stewed apple to the cheese mixture

Mrs J. Shute · North Humberside

Left: Welsh Rarebit. Right: Caerphilly Twist

Sweet 'n' Savoury Snack

4 slices of bread
English butter
4 rashers bacon, rinded and grilled
4 canned pear halves
175g (6oz) English Cheddar cheese, grated
parsley sprigs

1 Toast bread on one side only and spread other side with butter

2 Place a rasher of bacon on each slice of toast. Top with a pear half and then sprinkle evenly with cheese

3 Place under a hot grill until cheese has melted and turned golden brown. Garnish with parsley sprigs

Serves 4

For a variation replace the bacon and pears with ham and peaches

Mrs J. Birch · Blackpool

Caerphilly Twist

100g (4oz) Caerphilly cheese, grated
2–3 tablespoons fresh white breadcrumbs
1 egg, beaten
salt and freshly ground black pepper
Worcestershire sauce
1 cucumber, cut in half lengthways
215-g (7½-oz) packet frozen puff pastry, thawed
beaten egg

1 Mix 75g (3oz) cheese with breadcrumbs and bind with a little egg. Season with salt, black pepper and Worcestershire sauce

2 Sandwich the 2 cucumber halves together with the cheese mixture

3 Roll out the puff pastry to a rectangle on a lightly floured work top, and cut into strips 2·5cm (1 inch) wide. Wrap pastry strips around the cucumber, overlapping the edge a little like a cream horn case. Brush with egg and sprinkle with reserved cheese

4 Bake 220°C (425°F), mark 7, for 45 minutes. Serve hot

Serves 4–6

Courgettes could be used instead of the cucumber

Mrs J. Litster · Bath

Kentish Orchard Snack

1 onion, skinned and chopped
75g (3oz) English butter
150g (5oz) dessert plums, stoned and halved
salt and pepper
2 teaspoons sugar to taste
4 slices of bread
100g (4oz) Wensleydale or English Cheddar cheese,
　grated

1 Sauté onion in 25g (1oz) butter until soft but not
browned

2 Add plums and simmer until just soft but still whole

3 Season to taste and add just enough sugar to prevent
tartness

4 Toast the bread and spread with remaining butter

5 Divide plum mixture between slices and sprinkle with
cheese. Grill until golden and bubbling

Serves 2–4

Margaret S. Curran · Staplehurst

Cheddar Crusties

2 long bread rolls
100g (4oz) English Cheddar cheese, grated
½ onion, skinned and chopped
1 tomato, skinned and chopped
1–2 rashers bacon, rinded and chopped
salt and pepper
dash of milk
25g (1oz) fresh white breadcrumbs

1 Split the rolls and hollow out the centres. Toast the
outside crust of the rolls

2 Place cheese, onion, tomato, bacon, seasoning and
milk in a saucepan and stir over a low heat until cheese
melts

3 Fill the rolls with cheese sauce and place under a hot
grill until cheese bubbles. Sprinkle with breadcrumbs
and grill until golden brown. Serve with chutney and
salad

Serves 2

Janet Addia · Manchester

Mix grated Leicester cheese and crunchy peanut
butter with a little salt and pepper. Spread on to
hot toasted crumpets and reheat gently under the
grill. Serve hot for a tasty snack

Douglas Woodhouse-Rose · Chesterfield

Cheese Freiston

2 cooking apples, peeled, cored and chopped
2 onions, skinned and sliced
salt and pepper
225g (8oz) English Cheddar cheese, grated
225g (8oz) fresh white or brown breadcrumbs
50g (2oz) English butter
150ml (¼ pint) milk

1 Place half the apples in an ovenproof dish and cover
with half the onions; season to taste

2 Reserve 25g (1oz) of the cheese. Sprinkle half the
remaining cheese on top, followed by half the breadcrumbs. Dot with butter. Repeat the 4 layers. Pour on
milk and cover with foil

3 Bake 200°C (400°F), mark 6, for 40 minutes

4 Uncover and sprinkle with the reserved cheese

5 Bake for a further 20 minutes, reducing the
temperature to 190°C (375°F), mark 5, for the last 10
minutes

Serves 4–6

Mrs E. Smith · Boston

Cheese and Sesame Burgers

1 large onion, skinned and chopped
15g (½oz) English butter
1 large carrot, peeled and grated
2 tablespoons sesame seeds
175g (6oz) English Cheddar cheese, grated
450g (1lb) potatoes, cooked and mashed
salt and pepper
fine oatmeal

1 Fry onion in butter until soft but not browned

2 Mix with carrot, sesame seeds and 150g (5oz) of the
cheese into the potato and season well. Shape into
burgers

3 Mix sufficient oatmeal and remaining cheese and use
to coat the burgers

4 Fry in oil or grill until golden brown. Serve with green
salad or vegetables

Makes 10

Mrs Clare Neville · Linton

To make a tasty 'Cheese and Ginger snack', put a
generous helping of grated English Cheddar cheese
on to a slice of wholemeal toast and grill until
cheese has melted. Spread with ginger marmalade
and serve immediately

J. Caroline Bagshaw · Leeds

Savoury Flans

Quiches and savoury flans are ideal for so many occasions – lunches, suppers, picnics and parties, packed lunches and high teas. As they freeze well, the pastry cases can be made up in bulk and then filled with what ever is in store, together with cheese, of course!

Farmhouse Quiche

225g (8oz) shortcrust pastry made with 225g (8oz) plain flour (page 116)
1 onion, skinned and chopped
100g (4oz) streaky bacon, rinded and chopped
50g (2oz) mushrooms, sliced
25g (1oz) English butter
1 tablespoon sage and onion stuffing mix
213-g (7½-oz) can tomatoes, drained
175g (6oz) English Cheddar cheese, grated
100g (4oz) dessert apples, peeled and chopped
3 eggs, beaten
5 tablespoons milk
salt and pepper
1 teaspoon made English mustard
sprig of watercress

1 Make up shortcrust pastry (page 116)

2 Roll out pastry on a lightly floured work top and line a 23cm (9 inch) flan dish

3 Sauté onion, bacon, mushrooms in butter until soft

4 Stir in sage and onion stuffing mix and tomatoes. Allow to cool

5 Sprinkle half of the cheese over the base of flan, then spread the apple over followed by the sautéed mixture and the remaining cheese

6 Beat together the eggs, milk, seasoning to taste and mustard, and pour into flan

7 Bake 200°C (400°F), mark 6, for 50 minutes. Garnish with watercress and serve hot or cold

Serves 4–6

Mrs Gregory · Reigate

Left: Farmhouse Quiche. Right: Harvest Quiche

Harvest Quiche

225g (8oz) wheatmeal pastry made with 225g (8oz) wheatmeal flour (page 116)

1 small onion, skinned and chopped

225g (8oz) young courgettes, sliced thinly

25g (1oz) English butter

100g (4oz) button mushrooms, sliced

2 eggs, beaten

150ml (¼ pint) milk

225g (8oz) Lancashire cheese, grated

salt and pepper

dash of Worcestershire sauce

1 tomato, sliced

parsley sprig

1 Make up wholewheat pastry (page 116)

2 Roll out pastry on a lightly floured work top and line a 23cm (9 inch) flan ring

3 Fry the onion and courgettes in butter for 5 minutes. Add the mushrooms and continue to cook for a further 2 minutes

4 Beat the eggs and milk together, stir in the cheese, seasoning to taste and Worcestershire sauce

5 Place the cooked vegetables in the flan case and pour the egg mixture over. Arrange tomato on top

6 Bake 180°C (350°F), mark 4, for 50 minutes, until golden brown. Garnish with parsley and serve immediately

Serves 6

P. J. James · Chelmsford

Caerphilly Flan

175g (6oz) shortcrust pastry made with 175g (6oz) plain
   flour (page 116)
15g (½oz) English butter
2 sticks celery, finely chopped
2 tablespoons walnuts, crushed
75g (3oz) Caerphilly cheese, grated
2 eggs, beaten
150ml (5 fl oz) soured cream
salt and pepper
celery leaves

1 Make up three-quarters quantity shortcrust pastry
(page 116)

2 Roll out pastry on a lightly floured work top and line a
18cm (7 inch) flan ring. Prick the base

3 Bake 'blind' 200°C (400°F), mark 6, for 10 to 15
minutes

4 Melt butter and sauté the celery for 5 minutes. Spread
over the base of the flan and sprinkle with walnuts and
cheese

5 Beat eggs with the cream and season lightly

6 Bake 180°C (350°F), mark 4, for 40 to 45 minutes, or
until risen and golden brown. Garnish with celery leaves

Serves 4

Mrs Jill Foster · Brighton

Two Cheese Flan

175g (6oz) cheese pastry made with 175g (6oz) plain
   flour (page 116)
350g (12oz) minced beef
1 onion, skinned and chopped
50g (2oz) English butter
50g (2oz) mushrooms, chopped
2 tomatoes, skinned and chopped
salt and pepper
100g (4oz) Double Gloucester cheese, grated
25g (1oz) plain flour
300ml (½ pint) milk
watercress sprigs

1 Make up three-quarters quantity cheese pastry (page
116)

2 Roll out pastry on a lightly floured work top and line a
20·5cm (8 inch) flan ring

3 Fry beef and onion in 25g (1oz) butter until browned
and almost cooked. Add mushrooms, tomatoes and
seasoning to taste

4 Place half the mixture in the pastry case, sprinkle with
50g (2oz) cheese and top with the remaining meat
mixture

5 Bake 200°C (400°F), mark 6, for 20 minutes

6 Place flour, remaining butter and milk in a saucepan;
heat, stirring continuously, until the sauce thickens,
boils and is smooth. Cook for 1 minute

7 Remove pan from the heat, add remaining cheese and
stir, off the heat, until it has melted. Season to taste
with salt and pepper

8 Pour over the meat mixture and bake for a further 10
minutes. Serve hot garnished with watercress

Serves 4–6

Mrs J. M. Jeffs · Coventry

Gloucestershire Apple Flan

225g (8oz) shortcrust pastry made with 225g (8oz) plain
   flour (page 116)
2 cooking apples, peeled, cored and chopped
1 small onion, skinned and finely chopped
pinch of curry powder
¼ teaspoon grated nutmeg
50g (2oz) English butter
225g (8oz) Double Gloucester cheese, grated
3 eggs, beaten
300 ml (10 fl oz) fresh single cream
salt and freshly ground black pepper

1 Make up shortcrust pastry (page 116)

2 Roll out pastry on a lightly floured work top and line a
23cm (9 inch) flan ring. Prick the base

3 Bake 'blind' 200°C (400°F), mark 6, for 10 to 15
minutes

4 Cook apples, onion and spices in the butter in a
saucepan until soft, stirring all the time

5 Spread over the base of the flan, and sprinkle with
cheese

6 Beat eggs, fresh cream and seasoning to taste
together and pour over the cheese

7 Bake 180°C (350°F), mark 4, for 40 minutes. Serve hot

Serves 6

Mrs Margaret Taylor · Kendal

If a 'blind' baked pastry case has cracked or
collapsed at the edges, line the base and sides with
cheese before adding the filling. As the flan cooks
the cheese melts into the filling and also seals the
edges. Try using mild Caerphilly cheese for fruit
flans and English Cheddar or Cheshire cheese for
savoury flans

Mrs P. Austin · Walsall

Summer Cheese Flan

Summer Cheese Flan

225g (8oz) shortcrust pastry made with 225g (8oz) plain flour (page 116)
2 tablespoons water
1 heaped teaspoon gelatine
4 tablespoons milk
142g (5oz) natural yogurt
75g (3oz) English Cheddar cheese, grated
50g (2oz) cucumber, peeled and grated
salt and pepper
1 egg white
few slices of cucumber
pieces of red pepper

1 Make up shortcrust pastry (page 116)

2 Roll out pastry on a lightly floured work top and line a 20·5cm (8 inch) flan ring. Prick the base

3 Bake 'blind' 200°C (400°F), mark 6, for 10 to 15 minutes, then reduce temperature to 180°C (350°F), mark 4, for a further 15 minutes

4 Place cold water in a bowl and sprinkle in the gelatine. Stand the bowl over a saucepan of hot water and heat gently until dissolved. Allow to cool slightly

5 Mix milk and yogurt together and stir in the dissolved gelatine, cheese and cucumber. Season to taste with salt and pepper

6 Whisk the egg white until it stands in stiff peaks, fold into the cheese mixture and pour into the flan case. Allow to chill in the refrigerator. Garnish with cucumber and red pepper

Serves 4—6

Mrs D. M. Hodskinson · Birkenhead

Derbyshire Quiche

175g (6oz) wholemeal pastry made with 175g (6oz) wholemeal flour (page 116)
450g (1lb) onions, skinned and chopped
1 tablespoon vegetable oil
25g (1oz) English butter
2 eggs, beaten
2 tablespoons fresh single cream
1 teaspoon tarragon mustard
salt and freshly ground black pepper
100g (4oz) Sage Derby cheese, cubed

1 Make up three-quarters quantity wholemeal pastry (page 116)

2 Roll out pastry on a lightly floured work top and line a 20·5cm (8 inch) flan ring. Prick the base

3 Bake 'blind' 200°C (400°F), mark 6, for 10 to 15 minutes

4 Sauté the onions in oil and butter until soft, but not browned

5 Mix eggs with fresh cream, mustard and seasoning to taste

6 Add onions and pour into the flan case

7 Sprinkle cheese over the flan, and continue cooking for about 30 minutes, until set. Serve hot

Serves 4–6

This is delicious hot with salad or cold for picnics and hot or cold as a starter if divided into small flan dishes

Mrs Broadhurst · Wetherby

Watercress and Onion Flan

175g (6oz) shortcrust pastry made with 175g (6oz) plain flour (page 116)
1 medium onion, skinned and chopped
1 bunch watercress, washed, trimmed and finely chopped
100g (4oz) Red Windsor cheese, grated
2 eggs, beaten
150ml (¼ pint) milk
salt and pepper
watercress sprigs
onion rings
tomato slices

1 Make up three-quarters quantity shortcrust pastry (page 116)

2 Roll out pastry on a lightly floured work top and line a 18cm (7 inch) flan ring

3 Combine the chopped onion, watercress and 75g (3oz) of the cheese and place in the flan

4 Beat the eggs and milk together, season well and pour into the flan case

5 Sprinkle remaining cheese on top

6 Bake 200°C (400°F), mark 6, for 35 minutes. Garnish with watercress, onion rings and tomato slices. Serve hot or cold

Serves 4

Mrs J. W. Stacy · Hove

Broccoli and Cashew Flan

175g (6oz) shortcrust pastry made with 175g (6oz) plain flour (page 116)
40g (1½oz) plain flour
40g (1½oz) English butter
450ml (¾ pint) milk
salt
cayenne
100g (4oz) Lancashire cheese, crumbled
1 egg, separated
225g (8oz) broccoli, cooked and chopped
50g (2oz) cashew nuts, chopped

1 Make up three-quarters quantity shortcrust pastry (page 116)

2 Roll out pastry on a lightly floured work top and line a 20·5cm (8 inch) flan ring. Prick the base

3 Bake 'blind' 200°C (400°F), mark 6, for 10 to 15 minutes

4 Place the flour, butter and milk in a saucepan; heat, stirring continuously, until the sauce thickens, boils and is smooth. Cook for 1 minute. Season to taste with salt and cayenne

5 Remove pan from heat, add cheese and stir, off the heat, until it has melted. Stir in egg yolk

6 Whisk the egg white until it stands in stiff peaks and fold into the sauce

7 Place broccoli and nuts in the flan case and pour sauce on top, smoothing evenly

8 Bake 200°C (400°F), mark 6, for 30 minutes. Serve immediately

Serves 4–6

Mrs B. Hurst · Reading

Cheddar Cheese and Walnut Tart

175g (6oz) shortcrust pastry made with 175g (6oz) plain flour (page 116)
150ml (¼ pint) milk, boiling
50g (2oz) fresh white breadcrumbs
2 eggs, beaten
100g (4oz) English Cheddar cheese, grated
50g (2oz) walnuts, chopped
1 teaspoon Worcestershire sauce
few raw onion rings

1 Make up three-quarters quantity shortcrust pastry (page 116)

2 Roll out pastry on a lightly floured work top and line a 20·5cm (8 inch) flan ring. Prick the base

3 Bake 'blind' 200°C (400°F), mark 6, for 10 to 15 minutes

4 Pour the milk on to the breadcrumbs and infuse for 5 minutes

5 Beat well and add eggs, cheese, walnuts and Worcestershire sauce. Pour into the flan case

6 Bake 190°C (375°F), mark 5, for 30 minutes. Garnish with onion rings

Serves 4–6

Lillian Moorhouse · Bradford

Top left: Watercress and Onion Flan. Top right: Broccoli and Cashew Flan.
Bottom left: Derbyshire Quiche. Bottom right: Cheddar Cheese and Walnut Tart

49

Nut Brown Flan

175g (6oz) shortcrust pastry made with 175g (6oz) plain
    flour (page 116)
100g (4oz) granary breadcrumbs
100g (4oz) Leicester cheese, grated
100g (4oz) salted peanuts, coarsely chopped
3 tablespoons tomato chutney
2 eggs, beaten
300ml (½ pint) milk
slices of green pepper

1 Make up three-quarters quantity shortcrust pastry
(page 116)

2 Roll out pastry on a lightly floured work top and line a
20·5cm (8 inch) flan dish

3 Mix together breadcrumbs, cheese, peanuts, chutney,
eggs and milk. Place in the prepared flan case

4 Bake 190°C (375°F), mark 5, for 35 minutes

5 Garnish with green pepper

Serves 4–6

Mrs M Williams · Wigan

Cheese Sausage Flan

175g (6oz) shortcrust pastry made with 175g (6oz) plain
    flour (page 116)
225g (8oz) sausagemeat
2 eggs, beaten
1 small onion, skinned and finely chopped
½ level teaspoon dried mixed herbs
salt and pepper
100g (4oz) Double Gloucester cheese, grated
2 tomatoes, sliced

1 Make up three-quarters quantity shortcrust pastry
(page 116)

2 Roll out pastry on a lightly floured work top and line a
20·5cm (8 inch) flan dish, reserving some pastry for
strips

3 Using a fork, break up the sausagemeat. Add the
eggs, onion, mixed herbs and seasoning to taste. Pour
into the prepared flan case

4 Sprinkle cheese on top and arrange a lattice design
with reserved pastry strips; finish with slices of tomato

5 Bake 220°C (425°F), mark 7, for 30 to 35 minutes.
Serve hot or cold

Serves 4–6

Mrs Julia Proctor · Colchester

Cheese and Leek Flan

100g (4oz) cheese pastry made with 100g (4oz) plain
  flour (page 116)
450g (1lb) leeks, trimmed, cut in half lengthways and
  sliced
25g (1oz) English butter
150ml (5 fl oz) fresh double cream
1 egg yolk
100g (4oz) English Cheddar cheese, grated
¼ level teaspoon dried mixed herbs
salt and pepper

1 Make up half-quantity cheese pastry (page 116)

2 Roll out pastry on a lightly floured work top and line a
20·5cm (8 inch) flan dish

3 Fry the leeks in butter. Cool slightly and place in the
flan case

4 Mix fresh cream, egg yolk, cheese, mixed herbs and
seasoning to taste and pour into the flan

5 Bake 190°C (375°F), mark 5, for 35 to 40 minutes.
Serve immediately

Serves 4–6

Mrs G. S. Harrold · Caithness

Left to right: Nut Brown Flan, Cheese Sausage Flan, Cheese
and Leek Flan

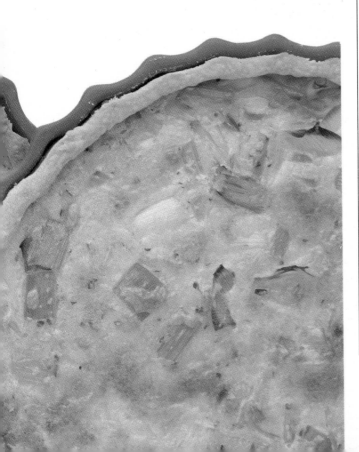

Pineapple and Cheddar Quiche

25g (1oz) English butter
5–6 large slices wholemeal bread, crusts removed
75g (3oz) pineapple pieces, drained if canned
100g (4oz) English Cheddar cheese, grated
2 eggs
150ml (¼ pint) milk
salt and pepper
tomato slices

1 Butter a 20·5cm (8 inch) flan dish. Butter the bread
and use to line the dish. Chill in the refrigerator for 30
minutes

2 Arrange the pineapple and cheese in the bread case

3 Beat together the eggs and milk, adding salt and
pepper to taste. Pour over the pineapple and cheese

4 Bake 190°C (375°F), mark 5, for 30 to 35 minutes until
firm and golden

5 Cool and garnish with tomato slices

Serves 4–6

Mrs A. M. Western · Isle of Man

Butterbean and Sage Derby Flan

175g (6oz) wholemeal pastry made with 175g (6oz)
  wholemeal flour (page 116)
1 large onion, skinned and chopped
50g (2oz) button mushrooms, chopped
25g (1oz) English butter
100g (4oz) butterbeans, soaked, cooked and drained
1 level teaspoon dry mustard
salt and freshly ground black pepper
150g (5oz) Sage Derby cheese, grated
1 egg, beaten
150ml (¼ pint) milk
fresh sage sprig

1 Make up three-quarters quantity wholemeal pastry
(page 116)

2 Roll out pastry on a lightly floured work top and line a
20·5cm (8 inch) flan ring

3 Sauté onion and mushrooms in butter, until soft.
Remove from the heat and stir in butterbeans, mustard
and seasoning to taste

4 Place in flan case and sprinkle with cheese

5 Mix egg and milk together and pour into flan

6 Bake 180°C (350°F), mark 4, for 30 to 35 minutes.
Garnish with fresh sage

Serves 4–6

Mrs M. S. Hanney · West Hampstead

51

Gower Flan

225g (8oz) shortcrust pastry made with 225g (8oz) plain flour (page 116)
15g (½oz) plain flour
40g (1½oz) English butter
150ml (¼ pint) milk
50ml (2 fl oz) dry white wine
75ml (3 fl oz) fresh single cream
salt and pepper
25g (1oz) shelled prawns
175–225g (6–8oz) laverbread or thawed frozen chopped spinach
275g (10oz) cockles in brine, drained
100g (4oz) Caerphilly cheese, grated
8 small croûtons
4 unshelled prawns

1 Make up shortcrust pastry (page 116)

2 Roll out pastry on a lightly floured work top and line a 23cm (9 inch) flan dish. Prick the base

3 Bake 'blind' 200°C (400°F), mark 6, for 10 to 15 minutes

4 Place the flour, butter and milk in a saucepan; heat, stirring continuously, until the sauce thickens, boils and is smooth. Stir in the white wine, fresh cream and seasoning to taste. Reheat gently and stir in the shelled prawns

5 Spread a good layer of laverbread or spinach (reserve some for the garnish) over the base of the flan and arrange cockles on top, reserving 8 for garnishing

6 Pour over the sauce and sprinkle with cheese

7 Bake 200°C (400°F), mark 6, for 15 minutes until golden brown

8 Spread a little of the remaining laverbread or spinach on each croûton and top with a reserved cockle. Use to garnish the flan together with the unshelled prawns. The croûtons and prawns can be dipped in a little aspic if desired and allowed to set firm before garnishing

Serves 4–6

Miss D. Davies · Llandeilo

Top to bottom: Gower Flan, Cheese and Smoked Mackerel Flan, Cheshire Tuna Fish Quiche

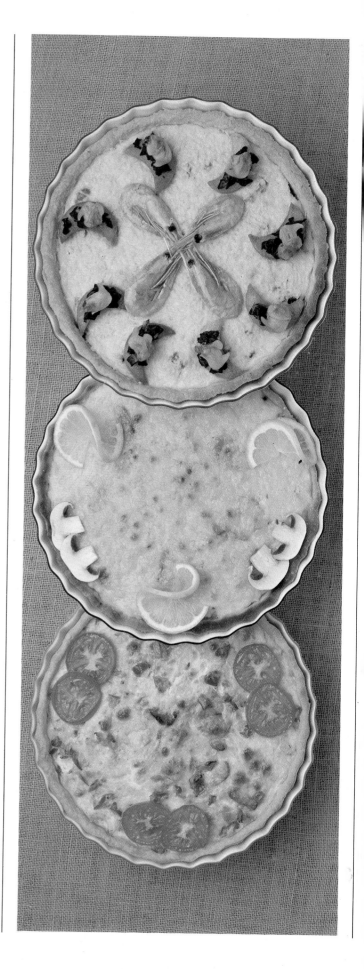

Cheese and Smoked Mackerel Flan

175g (6oz) shortcrust pastry made with 175g (6oz) plain flour (page 116)
100g (4oz) Cheshire cheese, grated
100g (4oz) smoked mackerel, bones and skin removed
142g (5oz) natural yogurt
150ml (5 fl oz) fresh single cream
2 eggs
1 teaspoon lemon juice
salt and pepper

1 Make up three-quarters quantity shortcrust pastry (page 116)

2 Roll out pastry on a lightly floured work top and line a 20·5cm (8 inch) flan ring

3 Liquidise cheese, smoked mackerel, yogurt, fresh cream, eggs, lemon juice and season to taste with salt and pepper. Pour into the flan case

4 Bake 200°C (400°F), mark 6, for 25 to 30 minutes. Serve hot or cold

Serves 4–6

If you do not have a liquidiser, flake the mackerel, and put alternate layers of mackerel and cheese in flan. Beat eggs with yogurt and milk and pour into the flan

Ann Johnson · Norwich

Cheshire Tuna Fish Quiche

225g (8oz) shortcrust pastry made with 225g (8oz) plain flour (page 116)
198-g (7-oz) can tuna in brine, drained and flaked
225g (8oz) Cheshire cheese, roughly grated
100g (4oz) prawns, peeled
1 green pepper, seeded and finely chopped
2 eggs, beaten
3 tablespoons milk
150ml (5 fl oz) fresh single cream
salt and pepper
2 tomatoes, sliced

1 Make up shortcrust pastry (page 116)

2 Roll out pastry on a lightly floured work top and line a 23cm (9 inch) flan dish

3 Fill with tuna, cheese, prawns and pepper

4 Beat eggs and milk, then stir in the fresh cream and seasoning to taste. Pour mixture into the flan

5 Garnish with tomato slices

6 Bake 200°C (400°F), mark 6, for 40 minutes. Serve hot

Serves 6

Miss J. M. Ward · North Berwich

Country Cheese Flan

175g (6oz) wholemeal pastry made with 175g (6oz) wholemeal flour (page 116)
198-g (7-oz) can sweetcorn, drained
1 small cauliflower, divided into florets and cooked
100g (4oz) English Cheddar cheese, grated
2 eggs
150ml (¼ pint) milk
salt and pepper

1 Make up three-quarters quantity wholemeal pastry (page 116)

2 Roll out pastry on a lightly floured work top and line a 18cm (7 inch) flan ring

3 Place the sweetcorn and cauliflower florets on the base of the flan. Sprinkle with cheese

4 Beat the eggs, milk and seasoning to taste together and pour over the vegetables

5 Bake 190°C (375°F), mark 5, for 30 minutes, until golden brown. Serve immediately

Serves 4

Mrs M. Cumming · Plymouth

Smoked Haddock Flan

100g (4oz) cheese pastry made with 100g (4oz) plain flour (page 116)
225g (8oz) smoked haddock, cooked and flaked
50g (2oz) button mushrooms, sliced
50g (2oz) English butter
198-g (7-oz) can sweetcorn, drained
300ml (½ pint) white sauce (page 116)
salt and pepper
50g (2oz) English Cheddar cheese, grated
twists of lemon
sprigs of parsley

1 Make up half-quantity cheese pastry (page 116)

2 Roll out pastry on a lightly floured work top and line a 18cm (7 inch) flan ring. Prick the base

3 Bake 'blind' 200°C (400°F), mark 6, for 10 to 15 minutes, then reduce temperature to 180°C (350°F), mark 4, for a further 15 minutes

4 Gently fry smoked haddock and mushrooms in butter for 1 to 2 minutes

5 Stir in sweetcorn, white sauce and seasoning to taste

6 Pour into the flan case and sprinkle cheese on top

7 Place under a hot grill for a few minutes until cheese has melted and is golden brown. Garnish with lemon and parsley. Serve hot

Serves 4

Mrs M. Wooler · High Wycombe

Cheese and Ham Flan

100g (4oz) cheese pastry made with 100g (4oz) plain
    flour (page 116)
300ml (½ pint) milk
40g (1½oz) fresh white breadcrumbs
100g (4oz) Double Gloucester or English Cheddar
    cheese, grated
50g (2oz) lean ham, chopped
2 eggs, beaten
salt and pepper
pinch of dry mustard (optional)
1 tomato, sliced

1 Make up half-quantity cheese pastry (page 116)

2 Roll out on a lightly floured work top and line a
18cm (7 inch) flan ring

3 Bring the milk to the boil and pour over the
breadcrumbs in a large bowl. Allow to cool slightly

4 Stir in the cheese, ham and eggs. Season with salt and
pepper to taste, plus a pinch of dry mustard if liked

5 Pour into the pastry case, and garnish with the tomato

6 Bake 200°C (400°F), mark 6, for 10 minutes, then
reduce temperature to 190°C (375°F), mark 5, for 15–20
minutes until golden brown. Serve hot

Serves 4

Mrs Rita Todd · Aylesbury

Cheese and Asparagus Quiche

225g (8oz) wholemeal pastry made with 225g (8oz)
    wholemeal flour (page 116)
200g (7oz) English Cheddar cheese, grated
100ml (4 fl oz) fresh single cream
75ml (3 fl oz) milk
3 eggs, beaten
salt and pepper
12 fresh asparagus tips, cooked and drained, or 280-g
    (10-oz) can asparagus tips, drained

1 Make up wholemeal pastry (page 116)

2 Roll out pastry on a lightly floured work top and line a
23cm (9 inch) flan ring

3 Sprinkle base of flan with 25g (1oz) of the cheese

4 Mix together the fresh cream, milk, eggs, remaining
cheese and season to taste. Pour into flan case

5 Arrange asparagus in a star formation on top

6 Bake 200°C (400°F), mark 6, for 30 to 35 minutes, until
filling is set. Serve hot or cold

Serves 6

Miss K. Fowler · Sheffield

Mediterranean Savoury Flan

225g (8oz) cheese pastry made with 225g (8oz) plain
    flour (page 116)
2 tablespoons vegetable oil
1 onion, skinned and sliced
2 garlic cloves, skinned and crushed
1 red pepper, seeded and sliced
1 small aubergine, chopped
225g (8oz) courgettes, sliced thinly
225g (8oz) tomatoes, skinned and chopped
salt and freshly ground pepper
150ml (¼ pint) water
1 level teaspoon dried oregano
225g (8oz) English Cheddar cheese, grated
50-g (1¾-oz) can anchovies, drained

1 Make up cheese pastry (page 116)

2 Roll out pastry on a lightly floured work top and line a
23cm (9 inch) flan ring. Prick the base

3 Bake 'blind' 200°C (400°F), mark 6, for 10 to 15
minutes

4 Heat oil and fry onion and garlic until soft, but not
browned

5 Add the remaining vegetables and seasoning to taste

6 Stir in the water, bring to the boil and simmer gently
for 30–40 minutes or until the juices are thick and
vegetables are tender. Stir occasionally

7 Remove from heat and stir in oregano and allow to
cool

8 Pour into the flan case

9 Sprinkle cheese on top and arrange anchovies in a
lattice design

10 Bake 200°C (400°F), mark 6, for 20 to 25 minutes,
until cheese is slightly browned. Serve hot or cold

Serves 6

Mrs Gibson · Braintree

Top: Vegetarian Cheese Flan. Bottom left and right:
Mediterranean Savoury Flan, Blue Stilton Pie

Vegetarian Cheese Flan

225g (8oz) shortcrust pastry made with 225g (8oz) plain flour (page 116)
450g (1lb) carrots, peeled and sliced
450g (1lb) swedes, peeled and chopped
50g (2oz) English butter
1 small onion, skinned and grated
salt and pepper
2 eggs, beaten
4 tablespoons milk
225g (8oz) English Cheddar cheese, grated
2 tomatoes, sliced
parsley sprigs

1 Make up shortcrust pastry (page 116)

2 Roll out pastry on a lightly floured work top and line a 25·5cm (10 inch) flan ring. Prick the base

3 Bake 'blind' 200°C (400°F), mark 6, for 10 to 15 minutes

4 Cook carrots and swedes in a saucepan of water until tender. Drain. Mash with the butter and onion. Season with salt and pepper to taste

5 Add eggs, milk, 50g (2oz) cheese to the vegetables in the pan, mix well and pour into the flan case

6 Sprinkle remaining cheese on top

7 Bake 190°C (375°F), mark 5, for 30 to 35 minutes. Garnish with tomato and parsley. Serve hot

Serves 6–8

Margaret Houldsworth · Congleton

Blue Stilton Pie

175g (6oz) shortcrust pastry made with 175g (6oz) plain flour (page 116)
100g (4oz) Blue Stilton cheese, crumbled
25g (1oz) full fat soft cheese
½ green pepper, seeded and chopped
1 tomato, skinned, seeded and chopped
2 eggs, beaten
150ml (5 fl oz) fresh single cream
salt and pepper
pinch of grated nutmeg

1 Make up three-quarters quantity shortcrust pastry (page 116)

2 Roll out pastry on a lightly floured work top and line a 20·5cm (8 inch) flan ring. Prick the base

3 Bake 'blind' 200°C (400°F), mark 6, for 10 to 15 minutes

4 Mash the cheeses together and add pepper and tomato

5 Stir eggs and fresh cream into the cheese and season to taste with salt, pepper and nutmeg. Pour into the flan case

6 Bake 180°C (350°F), mark 4, for 20 to 30 minutes. Serve hot or cold

Serves 4–6

Mrs Angela Pickering · Chester

Salads

For hot days or middays, salads can be more than just cheese salads. Incorporated with a variety of crunchy fruits or vegetables and enhanced with a tempting dressing; with crisp rolls or garlic bread, cheese gives the salad the place it deserves on the table.

 ## Circular Salad

150ml (¼ pint) cold water
15g (½oz) powdered gelatine
450ml (¾ pint) tomato juice
1 teaspoon Worcestershire sauce
1 teaspoon lemon juice
salt and pepper
100g (4oz) English Cheddar cheese, cubed
½ cucumber, cubed
100g (4oz) ham, cubed
75ml (2½ fl oz) fresh double cream, whipped
2 tablespoons mayonnaise
¼ level teaspoon curry powder
½ level teaspoon French mustard
½ level teaspoon grated onion
cress

1 Place the water in a small bowl and sprinkle in the gelatine. Stand the bowl over a saucepan of hot water and heat gently until dissolved. Leave to cool

2 When cool, mix with the tomato juice, Worcestershire sauce, lemon juice, and salt and pepper to taste. Pour into a damp ring mould and leave to set

3 Place the cheese, cucumber and ham in a bowl. Stir in the fresh cream, mayonnaise, curry powder, mustard and grated onion. Mix well and add salt and pepper to taste

4 Turn the tomato ring out on to a circular dish. Spoon the cheese mixture into the centre and around the edges of the ring. Garnish with cress

Serves 4—6

Mrs P. C. Marchant · Exeter

Left: Circular Salad. Right: Pineapple Cheese Moulds

Pineapple Cheese Moulds

4 radishes, thinly sliced
150ml (¼ pint) aspic jelly
397-g (13¼-oz) can crushed pineapple
pinch of salt
3 tablespoons cold water
15g (½oz) powdered gelatine
2 tablespoons lemon juice
100g (4oz) English Cheddar cheese, grated
150ml (5 fl oz) fresh double cream
tomato slices

1 Decorate the top of 8 dariole moulds or 6 yogurt cups with the thin slices of radish set in the aspic jelly

2 Heat the pineapple and add salt

3 Place the cold water in a bowl, sprinkle in the gelatine. Stand the bowl over a saucepan of hot water and heat gently until dissolved. Add to the hot pineapple mixture and stir until well mixed

4 Cool until the mixture begins to thicken, then add lemon juice and the grated cheese

5 Whip the fresh cream until softly stiff, fold into the mixture. Turn into the prepared moulds. Leave to set in a cool place

6 Turn out on to a serving plate and garnish with lettuce and tomato slices

Serves 4

Mrs Curtecka · Guildford

Cheese and Pasta Salad

175g (6oz) pasta shells
100g (4oz) English Cheddar cheese, diced
100g (4oz) Double Gloucester, diced
8 small gherkins, diced
1 small red pepper, seeded and diced
2 eggs, hard boiled and diced
142g (5oz) natural yogurt
1 tablespoon vinegar
1 level tablespoon sugar
salt and pepper
4 tablespoons milk

1 Boil pasta in salted water for 15 minutes then rinse well under cold water and drain

2 Mix together pasta, cheeses, gherkins, red pepper and hard-boiled eggs

3 Mix together yogurt, vinegar, sugar, salt and pepper to taste and milk. Pour over the other ingredients. Serve immediately

Serves 4

Mrs Barbara Ayre · Newcastle-upon-Tyne

Stir-fry Salad

4 tablespoons vegetable oil
225g (8oz) sprouted mung beans or bean sprouts
2 level teaspoons sesame seeds
450g (1lb) white cabbage, shredded
225g (8oz) carrots, peeled and coarsely grated
salt and pepper
175g (6oz) English Cheddar cheese, cubed
½ level teaspoon salt
½ level teaspoon cayenne
1½ tablespoons lemon juice

1 Heat 2 tablespoons of the oil in a large saucepan or wok and stir-fry the beans and sesame seeds for 4 minutes

2 Add the cabbage, carrots, salt and pepper and stir-fry for a further 3 minutes

3 Spoon into a serving bowl and stir in the cheese

4 Blend the remaining oil, salt, cayenne and lemon juice. Pour over the salad and toss well in the dressing

Serves 4–6

Mrs J. Patel · Wolverhampton

Cheese and Tuna Salad Flan

200-g (7-oz) can tuna, drained
175g (6oz) Double Gloucester cheese, grated
1 tablespoon salad cream
salt and pepper
1 medium lettuce, washed
¼ cucumber, sliced
4 radishes, sliced

1 Place the tuna into a bowl and mash. Stir in the cheese and salad cream. Mix well and add salt and pepper to taste

2 Line a 450g (1lb) loaf tin with greaseproof paper and spoon the mixture into it. Level the top and place a sheet of greaseproof paper over the top. Chill in the refrigerator

3 Arrange the lettuce on a serving plate. Remove the top greaseproof paper from the tuna and turn on to the lettuce. Peel off the remaining greaseproof paper

4 Arrange the cucumber slices and radishes on the sides and on top

5 Serve with salad and wholemeal bread or rolls

Serves 4

Salmon can be used in place of the tuna

Miss V. Howe · Leighton Buzzard

Fruity Fish Salad

100g (4oz) cooked pasta shells
1 small dessert apple, cored and diced
100g (4oz) green grapes, halved and seeded
50g (2oz) flaked almonds
2 celery sticks, chopped
175g (6oz) English Cheddar cheese, diced
142ml (5 fl oz) fresh double cream
2 tablespoons brown pickle
2 tablespoons mayonnaise
salt and pepper
225g (8oz) haddock, poached
chopped spinach

1 Place the pasta, apple, grapes, almonds, celery and cheese into a bowl

2 Whip the fresh cream until softly stiff and fold in the pickle and mayonnaise. Add salt and pepper to taste

3 Stir into the mixture and mix well

4 Flake the haddock, discarding any skin or bones, and stir into the mixture

5 Arrange spinach on a serving plate and spoon the salad on top

Serves 4

Eunice Petch · Wakefield

Lancashire Summer Salad

1 small lettuce, shredded
6 tomatoes, quartered
½ cucumber, sliced
1 onion, skinned and thinly sliced
1 green pepper, cored, seeded and sliced
2 tablespoons chopped fresh mint
1 tablespoon chopped fresh thyme
4 tablespoons olive or vegetable oil
2 tablespoons lemon juice
salt and pepper
175g (6oz) Lancashire cheese, thinly sliced
12 black olives

1 Arrange the lettuce in a serving bowl. Add the tomatoes, cucumber, onion and green pepper

2 Sprinkle with the mint and thyme

3 Blend together the oil, lemon juice, salt and pepper to taste and pour over the salad. Arrange the cheese and olives on top. Serve immediately

Serves 4–6

W. E. Grayburn · Thameshead

Cheesy Rice Salad

175g (6oz) long grain rice
425-g (15-oz) can red kidney beans, drained
200-g (7-oz) can pineapple cubes, drained
200-g (8-oz) can sweet corn, drained
1 green pepper, cored, seeded and sliced
1 red pepper, cored, seeded and sliced
2 celery sticks, chopped
225g (8oz) Double Gloucester cheese, diced
salt and freshly ground black pepper

1 Cook the rice in boiling salted water for 15 minutes or until tender. Drain, rinse and drain again

2 When cool place in a bowl with the kidney beans, pineapple, sweet corn, peppers, celery and cheese

3 Mix well and add salt and pepper to taste. Serve with rolls or garlic bread

Serves 4

French dressing may be served with the salad if wished

Mrs J. Chalkley · Barnsley

Olio Bowlio

100g (4oz) English Cheddar cheese, cubed
100g (4oz) bacon, chopped, fried and cooled
3 celery sticks, chopped
200-g (7-oz) can sweet corn, drained
50g (2oz) luncheon meat, diced
1 chicory head, sliced
75g (3oz) salted peanuts
142g (5oz) natural yogurt
1 teaspoon lemon juice
salt and pepper
lettuce

1 Place the cheese, bacon, celery, sweet corn, luncheon meat, chicory and peanuts in a bowl and toss together

2 Stir in the yogurt, lemon juice and salt and pepper to taste. Mix thoroughly

3 Arrange the lettuce on a serving plate and spoon the salad on top

Mrs P. C. Marchant · Exeter

Ham and Pear Salad

450g (1lb) ripe pears, peeled, cored and diced
100g (4oz) ham, diced
225g (8oz) Leicester cheese, grated
1 bunch watercress, washed, trimmed and chopped
142g (5oz) natural yogurt
2 teaspoons lemon juice
salt and freshly ground black pepper

1 Place the pears, ham, cheese and watercress in a bowl. Mix well

2 Stir in the yogurt, lemon juice and salt and pepper to taste. Toss well

3 Transfer to a serving dish and serve with crusty bread and green salad

Serves 4

If preferred, replace half the yogurt with salad cream or mayonnaise

Mrs L. Hodgson · Aldreth

Left: Fruity Fish Salad. Right: Cheesy Rice Salad

Cheese and Melon Salad

1 medium ripe Honeydew melon
100g (4oz) English Cheddar cheese, diced
1 dessert apple, peeled, cored and diced
25g (1oz) walnuts, chopped
100g (4oz) ham, cut into strips
142ml (5 fl oz) soured cream
2 tablespoons mayonnaise
¼ level teaspoon powdered ginger
salt and pepper
parsley sprig

1 Cut a zig-zag 'lid' from top of melon. Remove the melon flesh and cut into balls or cubes, then place in a bowl. Reserve the melon shell for serving the salad

2 Add the cheese, apple, walnuts and ham and mix well together

3 Stir in the soured cream, mayonnaise, ginger and salt and pepper to taste. Toss lightly together

4 Spoon the salad into the melon shell, and garnish with a parsley sprig

5 Chill in the refrigerator before serving. Serve with crusty rolls and a green salad

Serves 4

Any salad that does not fit into the shell can be served in a separate bowl

Mrs M. J. Smith · Winchmore Hill

Sunshine Salad

100g (4oz) Leicester cheese, grated
100g (4oz) Double Gloucester cheese, grated
312-g (11-oz) can mandarin oranges, drained
4 tablespoons finely grated carrot
1 tablespoon flaked almonds
2 tablespoons sultanas
chicory
4 tablespoons mayonnaise
grated rind and juice of 1 orange
1 level teaspoon tomato purée
2 teaspoons chopped fresh parsley
salt and pepper

1 Toss the cheeses, oranges, carrot, almonds and sultanas together in a large bowl

2 Arrange the chicory on a serving dish and spoon the salad on top

3 Mix together the mayonnaise, orange rind and juice, tomato purée, parsley, and salt and pepper to taste. Serve separately sprinkled with parsley

Serves 4

Marie Varndell · Portsmouth

Top: Sunshine Salad. Bottom left: Cheese and Melon Salad. Bottom right: Red Cabbage Salad

Chicory Salad

142g (5oz) natural yogurt
2 teaspoons honey
2 teaspoons lemon juice
1 level teaspoon French mustard
grated rind of ½ orange
225g (8oz) Leicester cheese, cubed
2 chicory heads, sliced
2 dessert apples, peeled, cored and chopped
2 oranges, peeled and segmented
chopped parsley

1 Blend together the yogurt, honey, lemon juice, mustard and orange rind

2 Place the cheese, chicory, apples and oranges in a bowl. Add the dressing and mix well

3 Spoon into a serving dish and sprinkle with chopped parsley

Serves 4

If chicory is not available, use 2 medium leeks, sliced and blanched in boiling water for 5 minutes. Drain and cool

Mrs V. Danvers · Lancaster

Red Cabbage Salad

1 medium red cabbage, shredded
4 tablespoons hot vinegar
lettuce
100g (4oz) streaky bacon, fried and crumbled
100g (4oz) Blue Stilton cheese, diced
1 tablespoon chopped fresh parsley
4 tablespoons vegetable oil
1 tablespoon vinegar
1 garlic clove, peeled and crushed
½ level teaspoon dried mixed herbs
¼ level teaspoon dry mustard
salt and freshly ground black pepper

1 Place the cabbage in a bowl and pour the vinegar over. Mix well

2 Cover the base and sides of a serving bowl with lettuce leaves. Spoon the cabbage on top

3 Sprinkle the bacon, cheese and parsley over the top

4 Blend the oil, vinegar, garlic, mixed herbs and dry mustard together, season to taste and pour over the salad. Serve with cold meats or sausage

Serves 6

G. A. Lacaruso · London W8

Cheese and Carrot Salad

175g (6oz) brown rice
2 carrots, peeled and grated
2 dessert apples, peeled, cored and chopped
salt and freshly ground black pepper
2 teaspoons honey
2 tablespoons orange juice
142ml (5 fl oz) fresh double cream, whipped
100g (4oz) English Cheddar cheese, cubed
50g (2oz) walnuts, chopped

1 Cook the rice in salted boiling water for 40 minutes or until tender. Drain, rinse and drain again

2 Place in a bowl and add the carrots, apples and salt and pepper to taste

3 Blend together the honey and orange juice. Fold in the whipped cream and mix into the rice with the cheese

4 Place in a serving bowl and chill for 30 minutes. Serve sprinkled with walnuts

Serves 4

Mrs M. Godfrey · Moulton

Cauliflower Salad

1 medium cauliflower, cooked and drained
142g (5oz) natural yogurt
100g (4oz) Blue Stilton cheese, crumbled
1 garlic clove, peeled and crushed
2 bacon rashers, chopped and cooked until crisp
1 small onion, finely chopped
salt and pepper
chopped parsley

1 Break the cauliflower into florets and place in a serving dish

2 Blend together yogurt, cheese and garlic. Stir in the bacon and onion, then add salt and pepper to taste

3 Pour over the cauliflower and garnish with parsley. Serve chilled

Serves 4

Mrs J. M. Kirkcaldy · Southampton

Lincs and Lancs Salad

1 clove garlic, peeled
50g (2oz) spinach, washed and torn
6 rashers bacon, fried and chopped
1 avocado, peeled and sliced
100g (4oz) Lancashire cheese, crumbled
4 spring onions, chopped
3 tablespoons chopped parsley
3 tablespoons vegetable oil
3 tablespoons lemon juice
salt and freshly ground black pepper
½ teaspoon sugar
½ level teaspoon dried mixed herbs
2 slices bread, crusts removed, cubed and fried

1 Rub a salad bowl with the garlic

2 Toss the spinach, bacon, avocado, cheese, spring onions and parsley together in the bowl

3 Mix the oil, lemon juice, salt and pepper, sugar and mixed herbs together and pour over the salad ingredients. Toss together

4 Add the croûtons just before serving

Serves 6

Mayonnaise

2 egg yolks
½ level teaspoon dry mustard
½ level teaspoon salt
½ level teaspoon caster sugar
¼ teaspoon Worcestershire sauce (optional)
pepper
300ml (½ pint) vegetable oil
2 tablespoons vinegar or lemon juice

1 Put yolks, mustard, salt, sugar, Worcestershire sauce (if used) and pepper into a bowl. Beat until smooth

2 Beating more quickly, add 150ml (¼ pint) oil, a drop at a time, and continue beating until mayonnaise is very thick

3 Stir in 1 tablespoon vinegar or lemon juice

4 Beat in rest of oil gradually, about 2 teaspoons at a time

5 When all the oil has been added, stir in last tablespoon of vinegar or lemon juice

6 Adjust seasoning to taste. Transfer to covered container. Serve with salads or ideal as a dip

Alternatively mayonnaise can be made using a liquidiser, which makes it much easier than beating it by hand. When adding the oil while making it in the liquidiser, it is advisable to pour the oil into the liquidiser bowl in a thin stream while the liquidiser is running

French Dressing

4 tablespoons olive oil
½ level teaspoon salt
½ level teaspoon icing or caster sugar
½ level teaspoon dry mustard
¼ teaspoon Worcestershire sauce
2 tablespoons vinegar or lemon juice

1 Beat oil, salt, sugar, mustard and Worcestershire sauce together

2 Gradually beat in vinegar or lemon juice until the dressing thickens

Blue Stilton Mayonnaise Dressing

1 egg yolk
½ level teaspoon salt
¼ level teaspoon paprika
1 level teaspoon icing sugar
pinch cayenne
½ level teaspoon mustard powder
3 tablespoons wine vinegar
1 tablespoon lemon juice
200ml (⅓ pint) vegetable oil
1 tablespoon boiling water
100g (4oz) Blue Stilton cheese, crumbled

1 Place the egg yolk, salt, paprika, sugar, cayenne, mustard, vinegar and lemon juice in a blender or food processor

2 Work until smooth, then gradually add the oil while the motor is running. Blend until the dressing has thickened

3 Add the water and blend until smooth. Stir in the cheese and spoon into a serving bowl. Serve with green salad, cold vegetables, fish, hard-boiled eggs or cold meats

Mrs B. M. Day · Doncaster

Yogurt Dressing

142g (5oz) natural yogurt
2 tablespoons fresh single cream
1 tablespoon lemon juice
1 level teaspoon icing or caster sugar
salt and pepper

1 Place yogurt into a bowl and blend in fresh cream, lemon juice and sugar. Season to taste with salt and pepper

2 Leave in a cool place for 15 minutes before using on salads or ideal for avocado with prawns

Soured Cream Dressing

150ml (5 fl oz) soured cream
1 tablespoon milk
1 tablespoon lemon juice or vinegar
½–1 level teaspoon icing or caster sugar
salt and pepper

1 Beat soured cream, milk, lemon juice or vinegar together

2 Stir in the sugar and season to taste with salt and pepper. Leave in a cool place for 15 minutes before using with salads or ideal for jacket potatoes

Blue Cheese Dressing

100g (4oz) full fat soft cheese
100g (4oz) Blue Stilton cheese
4 tablespoons mayonnaise
2 tablespoons natural yogurt
1 tablespoon milk
1 tablespoon chopped fresh parsley (optional)
1 tablespoon chopped fresh chives (optional)
1 garlic clove, crushed (optional)
15g (½oz) walnuts, finely chopped (optional)
1 teaspoon Worcestershire sauce (optional)

1 Place the soft cheese, Stilton and mayonnaise in a blender or food processor and work until smooth

2 Stir in the yogurt and milk

3 If liked stir in one of the additional ingredients. Spoon the dressing into a bowl and serve with a crisp green salad

Makes about 600ml (1 pint)

To make the dressing thinner, stir in extra milk

Mrs S. M. Neale · Keymer

Left to right: Yogurt Dressing, Blue Stilton Mayonnaise Dressing, Soured Cream Dressing

Picnics

These ideas are mainly for the 'moveable feast' but picnic dishes can be equally suitable for packed lunches for the children and as such are made more nutritionally sound with cheese. Some recipes give carrying and packing ideas – remember the value of cling film for keeping food fresh – vacuum flasks for keeping food hot or cold, as the case may be, and insulated boxes for the family picnic.

Date and Cheese Cakes

214-g (7 ½-oz) packet frozen puff pastry, thawed
100g (4oz) English Cheddar cheese, sliced
100g (4oz) dates, chopped
25g (1oz) walnuts, chopped
grated nutmeg
egg or milk

1 Roll out the pastry thinly on a lightly floured work top. Cut 4 circles 15cm (6 inches) diameter, using a saucer to cut around

2 In the centre of each circle place slices of cheese, dates, walnuts and a little grated nutmeg

3 Brush the edges of the pastry with water and pull together to enclose the filling. Shape into a cake and place join side down on a dampened baking sheet

4 Make slits in the top of each cake and brush with egg or milk

5 Bake 200°C (400°F), mark 6, for 15 to 20 minutes or until golden. Cool on a wire rack

Serves 4

Mrs V. Wareham · Melksham

Left: Date and Cheese Cakes.
Centre: Yummy Cheese Loaf.
Top right: Nutty Cheese Flapjacks.
Bottom right: Savoury Rock Cakes

Yummy Cheese Loaf

75g (3oz) English butter, softened
75g (3oz) caster sugar
1 egg, beaten
350g (12oz) self-raising flour, sifted
100g (4oz) English Cheddar cheese, grated
225g (8oz) mincemeat
150ml (¼ pint) milk
1 tablespoon rum or sherry (optional)

1 Place the butter and sugar in a bowl and cream together until pale and fluffy. Beat in the egg

2 Mix together the flour and cheese, then add half to the butter and sugar. Mix well

3 Stir in the mincemeat, then add the remaining flour and cheese with the milk and rum or sherry if used. Mix to a soft consistency

4 Spoon into a buttered 900g (2lb) loaf tin. Bake 170°C (325°F), mark 3, for 1 to 1½ hours or until cooked through. If the top is browning too quickly place a piece of foil over the top

5 Cool on a wire rack. Serve sliced with butter and cheese

Makes 15 slices

Mrs M. A. Dixon · Harrogate

Nutty Cheese Flapjacks

100g (4oz) rolled oats
75g (3oz) plain or wholemeal flour
50g (2oz) walnuts, finely chopped
½ level teaspoon dried mixed herbs
100g (4oz) English Cheddar cheese, grated
salt and pepper
75g (3oz) English butter
1 egg yolk
3–4 tablespoons milk

1 Place the oats, flour, nuts, herbs and grated cheese in a bowl and mix well. Add salt and pepper to taste

2 Melt the butter in a saucepan over a low heat. Allow to cool slightly, then add the egg yolk and mix well

3 Pour on to the dry ingredients with the milk and mix to make a moist consistency

4 Spread the mixture over the base of a buttered Swiss roll tin 27·5 × 20·5cm (11 × 8 inches)

5 Bake 190°C (375°F7, mark 5, for 25 to 35 minutes or until firm and golden. Cool slightly then cut into fingers or squares. Leave in the tin until cold

Serves 4–6

Mrs D. Fry · Beaminster

Savoury Rock Cakes

225g (8oz) self-raising flour
salt and pepper
100g (4oz) English butter
75g (3oz) English Cheddar cheese, grated
1 small onion, skinned and finely chopped
1 tomato, skinned and chopped
6 rashers streaky bacon, rinded and finely chopped
1 egg, beaten

1 Sift the flour into a bowl with salt and pepper to taste. Add the butter in pieces and rub into the flour until the mixture resembles fine breadcrumbs

2 Stir in the cheese, onion, tomato and bacon. Mix well

3 Add the egg and mix to a stiff dough. Place 12 to 14 mounds on a buttered baking sheet

4 Bake 190°C (375°F), mark 5, for 15 to 20 minutes or until firm and golden. Cool on a wire rack

Makes 12–14

Mrs A. D. Radley · Stoke-sub-Hamdon

Cheesy Nut Burgers

225g (8oz) finely ground nuts
50g (2oz) fresh breadcrumbs
100g (4oz) English Cheddar cheese, grated
1 medium onion, skinned and finely chopped
1 small carrot, peeled and grated
½ level teaspoon dry mustard
½ level teaspoon dried mixed herbs
salt and pepper
150ml (¼ pint) milk
1 egg, beaten
golden breadcrumbs
vegetable oil

1 Place the nuts, fresh breadcrumbs, cheese, onion, carrot, mustard, herbs, salt and pepper to taste in a mixing bowl

2 Mix well and bind with the milk

3 Divide into 8 and shape into burgers

4 Dip each burger in beaten egg, then roll in golden breadcrumbs to coat

5 Heat the oil in a shallow frying pan. Cook the burgers for 3 minutes on each side

6 Drain on absorbent kitchen paper and serve cold with mixed salad

Serves 4

Gillian Oakley · Kenilworth

Hot Tuna Burgers

200-g (7-oz) can tuna, drained
1 medium onion, skinned and finely chopped
100g (4oz) English Cheddar cheese, grated
50g (2oz) black olives, stoned and chopped
4 tablespoons mayonnaise
salt and freshly ground black pepper
6 soft rolls
English butter, softened

1 Place the tuna, onion, cheese, olives and mayonnaise in a bowl. Mix well and add salt and pepper to taste

2 Cut the rolls in half and spread with butter. Fill with the tuna mixture. Place in an ovenproof dish and cover with foil

3 Bake 180°C (350°F), mark 4, for 15 to 20 minutes. Serve hot or cold

Serves 4–6

Barbara Joan Massey · Colchester

Stilton Savoury Slice

370g (13oz) frozen puff pastry, thawed
1 egg, beaten
50g (2oz) English Cheddar cheese, grated
350g (12oz) cottage cheese
225g (8oz) Blue Stilton cheese, crumbled
4 tablespoons thick mayonnaise
100g (4oz) walnuts, chopped
1 onion, skinned and grated,
salt and freshly ground black pepper
watercress sprigs, washed and trimmed

1 Divide the pastry into two and roll out each piece on a lightly floured work top, to a rectangle 25·5 × 20·5cm (10 × 8 inches). Cut in half lengthways to give 4 rectangles 25·5 × 10cm (10 × 4 inches)

2 Place on a damp baking sheet. Brush with egg and sprinkle with Cheddar cheese

3 Bake 220°C (400°F), mark 7, for 15 to 20 minutes, until golden. Allow to cool

4 Mix cottage cheese, Stilton cheese, mayonnaise, nuts, onion, salt and pepper in bowl. Divide the mixture in half and spread on the base of two pastry slices. Sandwich with remaining two pastry slices. Serve garnished with watercress

Serves 6–8

Mrs Sharon Applewhite · Newark

Patio Pâté

100g (4oz) Leicester cheese, grated
100g (4oz) corned beef, chopped
1 small onion, skinned and finely chopped
garlic salt
freshly ground black pepper
Worcestershire sauce

1 Mash cheese, corned beef, onion, garlic salt and black pepper together

2 Moisten as necessary with Worcestershire sauce and press into a pâté mould or similar dish

3 Serve cold, on toast, as a filling for omelettes, toasted sandwiches or as a stuffing

Keith Carr-Glynn · Huntingdon

A versatile mixture which can be used as a spread for sandwiches and on biscuits, or as a dip with crisps, savoury biscuits and raw vegetables; can be made from grated Leicester cheese mixed with a little salad cream, chopped apple, celery, cucumber and seasoning

Douglas Woodhouse-Rose · Chesterfield

Picnic Rolls

4 large crusty rolls
225g (8oz) minced beef
1 medium onion, skinned and finely chopped
2 tablespoons tomato purée
100g (4oz) Wensleydale cheese, crumbled
1 level teaspoon dried oregano
salt and pepper

1 Cut the rolls in half. Scoop out the centre and make into crumbs

2 Place the crumbs in a bowl and add the minced beef, onion, tomato purée, cheese, oregano, and salt and pepper to taste

3 Mix well and use the mixture to fill the rolls. Wrap each one in foil and bake 200°C (400°F), mark 6, for 45 minutes

4 Open the foil and continue to cook for 5 to 10 minutes. Cool on a wire rack and serve cold with salad

Serves 4

Mrs Kareen Bunten · Dunfermline

Cheese Picnic Baskets

4 large crusty rolls
25g (1oz) English butter
1 dessert apple, cored and chopped
3 celery sticks, chopped
25g (1oz) sultanas
50g (2oz) Double Gloucester cheese, diced
50g (2oz) English Cheddar cheese, diced
salt and pepper
½ level teaspoon ground cinnamon
mayonnaise (optional)

1 Remove the tops from the rolls and scoop out some of the crumbs from the centre

2 Spread the top and bottom of each roll with the butter

3 Place the apple, celery, sultanas and cheeses in a bowl. Add salt and pepper to taste and the cinnamon

4 Toss well together and use to fill the rolls. Serve with mayonnaise separately if liked

Serves 4

Susan Gibson · Bradford

Left: Picnic Rolls. Right: Cheese Picnic Baskets

Cheese and Gammon Puffs

25g (1oz) English butter
25g (1oz) plain flour
150ml (¼ pint) milk
100g (4oz) gammon, minced
100g (4oz) mature English Cheddar cheese, grated
1 tablespoon chopped fresh parsley
salt and pepper
cayenne
214-g (7½-oz) packet frozen puff pastry, thawed
egg or milk

1 Place the butter, flour and milk in a saucepan. Heat, stirring continuously until the sauce thickens, boils and is smooth. Cool for 1 minute. Remove from the heat

2 Stir in the gammon, cheese, parsley, salt, pepper and cayenne, then leave to cool

3 Roll out the pastry thinly and cut 4 circles 15cm (6 inches) diameter, using a saucer to cut around

4 Divide the filling between the pastry circles. Brush the edges with water and fold over to make a pasty shape. Knock the edges together to seal

5 Make a hole in the top of each puff and, if liked, decorate the top with pastry leaves. Brush with egg or milk and place on a dampened baking sheet

6 Bake 220°C (425°F), mark 7, for 15 minutes, then lower the temperature to 190°C (375°F), mark 5, for 10 minutes. Cool on a wire rack

Serves 4

Mrs M. Witts · Guildford

Ploughman's Porky Loaf

3 rashers bacon, rinded
450g (1lb) lean pork (spare rib or cut from shoulder)
1 medium onion, skinned
3 tablespoons chopped fresh sage or 2 level teaspoons dried sage
salt and pepper
100g (4oz) stale brown bread
300ml (½ pint) chicken stock
1 dessert apple, peeled and grated
175g (6oz) pork sausagemeat
175g (6oz) mature English Cheddar cheese, grated
3 tablespoons chopped fresh parsley
1 level teaspoon dried thyme
6 to 8 button mushrooms, wiped
slices of cucumber and tomato

1 Butter a 900g (2lb) loaf tin and line with the bacon

2 Mince the pork and onion in a food processor or mincer. Stir in the sage, salt and pepper to taste

3 Soak the bread in the stock in a bowl for 30 minutes. Add the apple, sausagemeat, cheese, parsley and thyme. Mix well and add a little salt and pepper to the stuffing mixture

4 In the prepared tin place half the minced pork, then spoon the stuffing over and level with a knife. Slice the mushrooms and lay them on the stuffing

5 Place the remaining pork on top and cover with foil

6 Place the tin in a roasting pan containing a little water. Bake 170°C (325°F), mark 3, for 1½ to 1¾ hours

7 Remove from the oven and drain off the excess liquid. Leave to cool, then place in the refrigerator with a weight on top for 2 to 3 hours

8 Turn out the loaf and garnish with cucumber and tomato slices. Serve cut into slices

Serves 6–8

Mrs Q. Newcombe · South Molton

Savoury Plaits

214-g (7½-oz) packet frozen puff pastry, thawed
2 level teaspoons made mustard (optional)
3 level tablespoons sage and onion stuffing mix
100g (4oz) Leicester cheese, grated
450g (1lb) sausagemeat
milk for brusning

1 Divide the pastry into two and roll out each piece on a lightly floured work top to a rectangle. Spread the mustard, if used, down the centre of each

2 Mix together the stuffing mix and cheese and sprinkle down the centre of each piece of pastry

3 Divide the sausagemeat into two and make into rolls the same length as the pastry. Place each roll on top of the stuffing mixture

4 Cut pastry with a sharp knife to form diagonal strips each side of the sausagemeat. Brush the pastry strips with milk, then fold over the filling to form a plait. Repeat with the other roll

5 Place the plaits on a baking sheet and brush the pastry with milk

6 Bake 230°C (450°F), mark 8, for 30 to 40 minutes or until cooked and golden. Cool on a wire rack. Serve cut into slices

Serves 4–6

Mrs M. Jones · Llanfairpwll

Top left: Cheese and Gammon Puffs, Savoury Plaits. Bottom left: Savoury Cheesecake. Top right: Cheese and Lentil Loaf. Right: Ploughman's Porky Loaf

Savoury Cheesecake

100g (4oz) bran biscuits or savoury crackers
50g (2oz) English butter, melted
225g (8oz) English Cheshire cheese, grated
225g (8oz) natural cottage cheese, sieved
50g (2oz) ham or salami, finely chopped
2–3 spring onions, trimmed and finely chopped
50g (2oz) salted peanuts, crushed
salt and freshly ground black pepper

1 Crush biscuits and mix with the melted butter. Press into the base of an 18cm (7 inch) loose-bottomed cake tin

2 Mix together the Cheshire cheese and cottage cheese. Add the ham or salami and spring onions. Mix well

3 Stir in half the peanuts with salt and pepper to taste

4 Spread the mixture over the biscuit base and chill in the refrigerator

5 Remove the cheesecake from the tin and place on a serving plate. Sprinkle the remaining peanuts on top

Serves 6–8

Mrs H. Marshall · Stockport

Cheese and Lentil Loaf

1 tablespoon vegetable oil
1 large onion, skinned and sliced
225g (8oz) lentils
2 level tablespoons dried mixed vegetables
200-g (14-oz) can tomatoes
1 tablespoon tomato purée
150ml (¼ pint) water
50g (2oz) mushrooms, chopped
2 eggs, beaten
100g (4oz) Leicester cheese, grated
100g (4oz) fresh brown breadcrumbs
2 level teaspoons dried thyme
salt and pepper
slices of green pepper

1 Heat the oil in a large saucepan and fry the onion until soft

2 Add the lentils, mixed vegetables, tomatoes with their juice, tomato purée and water. Bring to the boil, cover and simmer for 30 minutes or until the lentils are soft. Allow to cool slightly

3 Stir in the mushrooms, eggs, cheese, breadcrumbs, thyme, and salt and pepper to taste. Mix well and spoon into a buttered 900g (2lb) loaf tin

4 Bake 180°C (350°F), mark 4, for 1 hour. Turn on to a serving plate and serve cut into slices with salad garnished with slices of green pepper

Serves 8

Mrs R. Joseph · Cardiff

Cheddar Sunset Loaf

2 eggs, beaten
100g (4oz) Double Gloucester cheese, grated
25g (1oz) fresh breadcrumbs
½ level teaspoon dried oregano
½ teaspoon soy sauce
1 small onion, skinned and chopped
salt and pepper
175g (6oz) self-raising flour
2 large tomatoes
75g (3oz) English Cheddar cheese, sliced

1 Mix together the eggs, cheese, breadcrumbs, oregano, soy sauce, onion, and salt and pepper to taste

2 Work in the flour a little at a time to make a soft dough. Knead well and divide into 2 pieces

3 Place 1 piece in the base of a buttered 450g (1lb) loaf tin. Skin and slice the tomatoes and place over the dough

4 Arrange the cheese slices on the tomatoes and top with the remaining dough

5 Bake 180°C (350°F), mark 4, for 40 to 45 minutes or until firm and golden. Cool on a wire rack. Serve sliced with butter

Makes about 10 slices

Janet M. McLarty · Tonbridge

Cheese and Garlic Loaf

225g (8oz) plain flour
200g (7oz) wholemeal flour
2 level teaspoons baking powder
50g (2oz) English butter
175g (6oz) English Cheddar cheese, grated
1 garlic clove, skinned and crushed
1 egg, lightly beaten
300ml (½ pint) milk

1 Mix the plain and wholemeal flour together in a bowl with the baking powder. Add the butter, cut into pieces, and rub it in until the mixture resembles fine breadcrumbs

2 Add the cheese and garlic, then stir in the egg and milk to form a soft dough. Knead lightly and place in a well buttered, 900g (2lb) loaf tin

3 Bake in the oven at 200°C (400°F), mark 6, for about 50 minutes, until risen and browned on top

4 Cool on a wire rack, then serve buttered

Makes a 900g/2lb loaf

This bread makes delicious tomato sandwiches

Mrs J. M. Skipsey · Norwich

Sandwich Fillings

The sandwich is generally a well used but most underrated dish. With a well chosen filling, generous amounts of English butter and an interesting bread it is no longer the much maligned 'doorstep' but is a nutritious and delicious meal in itself. Ready in a moment, easily packed and eaten anywhere, here are a few sandwich filling ideas to liven up any packed lunch, picnic or snacktime.
Simply combine the ingredients together and spread generous amounts onto well buttered bread. Ready prepared fillings can be kept in the refrigerator for several days, and used as required.

Liver Sausage and Cheese Spread

100g (4oz) Leicester cheese, grated
50g (2oz) liver sausage, mashed
1 tablespoon finely chopped cucumber

Country Cheese and Ham Spread

100g (4oz) Wensleydale cheese, grated
50g (2oz) ham, chopped
25g (1oz) English butter, softened
1 tablespoon milk
1 tablespoon chopped chives

Crunchy Cheese Spread

100g (4oz) Lancashire cheese, grated
1 apple, chopped
1 stick celery, chopped
2 tablespoons natural yogurt

Hawaiian Delight

100g (4oz) Caerphilly cheese, grated
4 tablespoons top of the milk
50g (2oz) pineapple, chopped

Fruity Cheese Spread

100g (4oz) Cheshire cheese, grated
1 banana, mashed
2 teaspoons lemon juice
25g (1oz) sultanas
1 tablespoon fresh single cream

Cheese and Tuna Spread

100g (4oz) Double Gloucester cheese, grated
90-g (3½-oz) can tuna fish, drained and flaked
2 tablespoons salad cream
salt and pepper

Top: Cheddar Sandwich Spread. Bottom left: Lancashire, Date and Walnut Spread.
Bottom right: Red Windsor and Watercress Spread

Lancashire, Date and Walnut Spread

100g (4oz) Lancashire cheese, crumbled
4 dates, chopped
12g (½oz) walnuts, chopped
3 tablespoons natural yogurt

Red Windsor and Watercress Spread

100g (4oz) Red Windsor cheese, grated
2 tablespoons finely chopped watercress
3 tablespoons fresh cream
salt and pepper

Cheese 'n' Beef Spread

100g (4oz) Leicester cheese, grated
75g (3oz) corned beef, mashed
2 tablespoons tomato ketchup

Cheddar Sandwich Spread

100g (4oz) English Cheddar cheese, grated
25g (1oz) English butter, softened
2 tablespoons sandwich spread
3 spring onions, finely chopped

Cheese and Egg Spread

100g (4oz) Double Gloucester cheese, grated
1 egg, hard boiled and mashed
2 tablespoons salad cream

Cheese 'n' Chicken Spread

100g (4oz) Sage Derby cheese, grated
75g (3oz) cooked chicken, shredded
2 tablespoons mayonnaise

Cheesy Peanut Spread

100g (4oz) English Cheddar, grated
50g (2oz) peanut butter, crunchy or smooth

For a delicious sandwich filling, combine a small
can of butter beans, 100g (4oz) grated English
Cheddar cheese, 15g (½oz) English butter,
2 tablespoons of milk and season to taste with salt,
freshly ground black pepper and a little made
mustard

Veronica McGlone · Chorlton-cum-Hardy

Open Sandwiches

Whether for a special occasion picnic, a lunch in the garden, high tea or as a quick refreshment for friends, open sandwiches make an appealing and appetizing snack.

Quick and easy to prepare they can be packed into rigid plastic containers or wrapped in cling film for transportation.

Crusty white, brown or rye bread spread generously with English butter and topped with any of the following suggestions are irresistible to the eye as well as the palate

'Cheddar Gorge-ous'

Slice of English Cheddar cheese and two frankfurters garnished with a little mayonnaise and mustard mixed together, a crisp lettuce leaf, red pepper strips and parsley

'Walton upon the Thames'

Cubes of Walton cheese, diced celery, apple and walnuts mixed with a little mayonnaise garnished with crisp lettuce and slices of kiwi fruit

'On the Dales'

Slices of Wensleydale cheese, topped with two folded slices of ham, garnished with a twist of orange and a little cress

'At the Derby'

Overlapping slices of pork and Sage Derby topped with a ring of apple soaked in lemon juice and garnished with a sprig of watercress

'On Safari'

Shredded cooked chicken, topped with grated Windsor Red cheese and a little cranberry sauce

'In the Forest'

A bed of shredded crispy lettuce topped with cubes of corned beef and grated Sherwood cheese, garnished with tomato slices

'A hunting we will go'

Cubes of Huntsman cheese and apple mixed with a little fresh cream or natural yogurt, garnished with slices of apple dipped in lemon juice

'In the Hills'

Slices of Cheviot cheese topped with chopped celery and crispy bacon

Top left: 'On the Dales'. Top right: 'Cheddar Gorge-ous'. Bottom left: 'At the Derby'. Bottom right: 'Walton upon the Thames'

'Leicester Races'

Crispy lettuce topped with a mixture of grated Leicestershire cheese and a little fresh cream, garnished with chopped dates

'Dr Foster went to . . .'

Slices of Double Gloucester cheese topped with alternate slices of cucumber and tomato, and a little pickle across the top

'Finding the route to Rutland'

Slices of Rutland cheese, topped with shredded lettuce, some slices of pickled onion and chopped celery. Garnished with a little mayonnaise, a twisted slice of tomato sprinkled with some chopped parsley

'Cheshire Cat'

Crisp lettuce topped with finely grated Cheshire cheese and fresh pear slices

'And so to Wales'

Slices of Caerphilly cheese topped with rings of cooked leeks. Garnished with some natural yogurt with paprika and a few chopped chives

'The way of the Wolds'

Slices of Cotswold cheese topped with coleslaw and slices of liver sausage. Garnished with watercress and some grated carrot sprinkled over the top

Dinner Parties

Cheese finds its way into all courses at a dinner party, whether as an integral part – for flavour; as a topping – for colour and texture; or as a course by itself – the cheese board. Cheese combines well with meat, fish, eggs and vegetables, and gives variety to basic ingredients.

 ## Chicken Sage Derby

4 boned chicken breasts
150g (5oz) Sage Derby cheese, grated
75g (3oz) English butter, softened
25g (1oz) streaky bacon, rinded and cut into small strips
pinch of dried sage
4 wooden cocktail sticks
50g (2oz) plain flour
1 egg, beaten
toasted breadcrumbs
1 tablespoon vegetable oil
watercress sprigs

1 Skin the chicken breasts and place in a wet polythene bag and beat with a rolling pin, until flattened

2 Mix cheese, 50g (2oz) of the butter, bacon and sage together and divide between pieces of chicken

3 Roll up neatly and secure with a wooden cocktail stick

4 Toss in flour, brush with egg and coat in breadcrumbs. Allow to chill

5 Sauté in remaining butter and oil until golden. Transfer to an ovenproof casserole

6 Bake 190°C (375°C), mark 5, for 20 to 30 minutes. Garnish with watercress

Serves 4

P. Carmody · Sidcup

Leicestershire Pâté

75g (3oz) English butter
1 large onion, skinned and finely chopped
2 garlic cloves, skinned and crushed
350g (12oz) button mushrooms, finely chopped
450g (1lb) carrots, grated
225g (8oz) Leicester cheese, grated
100g (4oz) ground almonds
4 eggs, beaten
1 tablespoon chopped fresh parsley
1 level teaspoon dried thyme
½ level teaspoon dried oregano
1 tablespoon lemon juice
salt and freshly ground pepper
bunch of watercress, washed and trimmed

1 Melt the butter in a frying pan. Add the onion and garlic and fry until soft but not browned — about 5 minutes

2 Add the mushrooms and stir over the heat until most of the juices have evaporated. Stir the mixture frequently to make sure it does not stick to the pan

3 Cool slightly, then reduce the onion and mushroom mixture to a smooth purée in a liquidiser or food processor. Transfer to a large mixing bowl

4 Add all the remaining ingredients except the watercress and mix well. Taste and add seasoning, then spoon the pâté into a buttered 900g (2lb) loaf tin

5 Stand the loaf tin in a roasting tin and add hot water to come almost to the rim of the outer tin. Bake in the oven at 180°C (350°F), mark 4, for 1½ hours, or until a skewer inserted in the centre comes out clean

6 Chill well and turn out on to a serving dish. Garnish with watercress and serve with wholemeal toast or bread

Serves 10–12

Mrs M. Taylor · Kendal

Left to right: Chicken Sage Derby, Leicestershire Pâté, Shrimp Horns

Shrimp Horns

215-g (7 ½-oz) packet frozen puff pastry, thawed
a little milk
15g (½oz) plain flour
15g (½oz) English butter
150ml (¼ pint) milk
75g (3oz) English Cheddar cheese, grated
salt and pepper
¼ level teaspoon made mustard
150ml (¼ pint) fresh or frozen peeled shrimps, chopped
1 teaspoon chopped parsley
16 to 18 whole shrimps
parsley sprigs

1 Roll out pastry on a floured work top and cut into strips 30·5cm (12 inches) long and 1cm (½ inch) wide

2 Brush one edge of each strip with water and wind round a cream horn tin, starting at the tip and overlapping the dampened edges. Place on a damp baking sheet with the join underneath

3 Bake 220°C (425°F), mark 7, for 10 minutes. Remove from the oven and brush with a little milk, return to the oven for a further 5 to 10 minutes

4 Leave to cool for a few minutes then carefully remove pastry from the horn tins

5 Place the flour, butter and remaining milk in a saucepan, heat stirring continuously until the sauce thickens, boils and is smooth. Cook for 1 minute

6 Remove from the heat, add cheese and stir off the heat until it has melted. Season to taste with salt, pepper and mustard. Stir in the chopped shrimps and parsley

7 Fill each pastry horn with the shrimp sauce and garnish with whole shrimps and parsley

Makes 12

Mrs P. Chamberlain · Norwich

Fillet of Brill Gloucester Style

4 × 100–125g (4–5oz) fillets of brill, skinned, or cod, lemon sole or plaice fillets
salt and freshly ground black pepper
25g (1oz) plain flour
25g (1oz) English butter, melted
225g (8oz) Double Gloucester cheese, coarsely grated
1½ tablespoons mild Dijon mustard
3–4 tablespoons fresh double cream
a little dry white wine or vermouth (optional)

1 Season the fish with salt and toss in flour to coat evenly all over. Melt the butter in an ovenproof dish and place the fish on top

2 Mix the cheese, mustard, fresh cream, pepper and wine, if used, into a smooth paste. Spread evenly over the fish

3 Bake 180°C (350°F), mark 4, for 20 to 30 minutes, taking care not to over-brown the cheese. Serve immediately

Serves 4

Konrad R. Hollies · St Martins

Shrimp Circle

15g (½oz) gelatine
300ml (½ pint) milk
250ml (8 fl oz) soured cream
3 tablespoons dry white wine
1 teaspoon grated lemon rind
1 teaspoon lemon juice
1 teaspoon Worcestershire sauce
½ teaspoon chopped chives
½ level teaspoon salt
275g (10oz) Tokay or sweet grapes, halved and pipped
175g (6oz) peeled shrimps
1 small green pepper, seeded and finely chopped
100g (4oz) Wensleydale cheese, grated
crisp lettuce leaves
a few whole shrimps (optional)

1 Place 2 tablespoons cold water in a small bowl and sprinkle in the gelatine. Stand the bowl over a saucepan of hot water and heat gently until dissolved

2 In a large bowl mix together the dissolved gelatine, milk, soured cream, wine, lemon rind and juice, Worcestershire sauce, chives and salt. Leave in a cool place until the mixture is beginning to set

3 Fold in the grapes, shrimps, green pepper and cheese. Pour into a 20·5cm (8 inch) ring mould and chill until firm

4 To serve, dip the mould in hot water, wipe the outside, then invert on to a round platter. Garnish with crisp lettuce leaves and a few whole shrimps, if liked

Serves 4–6

Miss E. M. R. Noble · Carshalton Beeches

Smoked Haddock Roulade

450ml (¾ pint) milk
1 carrot, peeled
1 onion, skinned and halved
1 bay leaf
65g (2½oz) English butter
40g (1½oz) plain flour
salt and freshly ground black pepper
1–2 teaspoons anchovy essence
225g (8oz) smoked haddock, poached and flaked
4 eggs, separated
100g (4oz) English Cheddar cheese, very finely grated
50g (2oz) peeled prawns
50g (2oz) mushrooms
2 eggs, hard-boiled and grated

1 Place the milk in a saucepan with the carrot, onion and bay leaf. Bring to the boil, remove from the heat and leave to infuse for 30 minutes

2 Melt 40g (1½oz) of the butter and stir in the flour and cook for 1 to 2 minutes

3 Strain the milk and gradually add to the pan; heat, stirring continuously until the sauce thickens, boils and is smooth. Cook for 1 minute. Stir in the seasoning and anchovy essence to taste

4 Mix 3 tablespoons of the sauce with the fish, egg yolks and 75g (3oz) of the cheese

5 Whisk the egg whites and fold into the fish mixture. Pour into a lined and well-buttered 32 × 23cm (13 × 9 inch) Swiss roll tin

6 Bake 200°C (400°F), mark 6, for 15 to 20 minutes

7 Sauté the prawns and mushrooms in remaining butter for 1 to 2 minutes and add to the remaining sauce with the hard-boiled eggs

8 Turn the roulade out on to a sheet of greaseproof paper resting on a folded tea towel; remove the paper lining. Spread sauce over the roulade and carefully roll up, like a Swiss roll, using the greaseproof paper to roll it evenly. Sprinkle with remaining cheese and serve immediately

Serves 4–6

Belinda Sweeting · Bristol

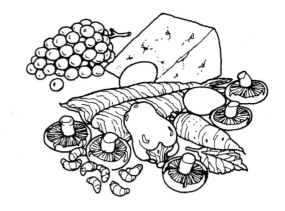

Blue Stilton and Grape Mousse Everglade

3 egg yolks
150ml (5 fl oz) fresh single cream
150ml (5 fl oz) warm water
15g (½oz) gelatine
125g (4oz) white grapes, skinned, pipped and halved
125g (4oz) black grapes, skinned, pipped and halved
2 teaspoons chopped fresh mint
pinch of paprika
100g (4oz) Blue Stilton cheese, finely chopped
salt and freshly ground pepper
300ml (10 fl oz) fresh double cream
bunch of cress, washed and trimmed

1 Mix the egg yolks with the fresh single cream in a basin. Stand the basin over a pan of gently simmering water and cook, stirring continuously, until thickened. Do not allow the water to boil or the egg yolks will curdle. Remove the pan from the heat

2 Place 5 tablespoons of the measured water in a small bowl and sprinkle in the gelatine. Stand the bowl over a saucepan of hot water and heat gently until dissolved. Add remaining water. Leave to cool

3 Pour boiling water over 75g (3oz) each of the white and black grapes. Skin, halve and remove pips

4 Stir the gelatine into the egg mixture together with the peeled grapes, mint, paprika, cheese and seasoning to taste and mix well. Leave in a cool place until half set

5 Whip the fresh double cream until softly stiff and fold into the mixture

6 Pour the mixture into a wetted 20·5cm (8 inch) ring mould, return to the refrigerator and chill until set, about 1–2 hours

7 Dip the mould quickly in hot water, wipe the outside and invert on to a serving dish or plate

8 Halve remaining white and black grapes and remove the pips. Arrange alternatively on top of the mould. Fill the centre of the mould with cress. Keep chilled until ready to serve

Serves 8

Mr N. A. Johnson · Blackpool

Left: Smoked Haddock Roulade. Right: Blue Stilton and Grape Mousse Everglade

Pork Fillet en Croûte

450g (1lb) pork fillet
25g (1oz) English butter
50–75g (2–3oz) Blue Stilton cheese, sliced
salt and freshly ground pepper
215-g (7½-oz) packet frozen puff pastry, thawed
1 egg, beaten
watercress sprigs

1 Fry the pork fillet in butter until sealed and golden

2 Drain on absorbent kitchen paper and allow to cool

3 Make a slit down the edge of the meat and fill with slices of cheese. Season the meat all over

4 Roll out pastry into an oblong large enough to enclose the meat. Place the meat in the centre of the pastry and fold the edges over. Seal with a little egg and place on a damp baking sheet with the join underneath

5 Decorate with pastry leaves and brush all over with egg

6 Bake 220°C (425°F), mark 7, for 45 to 50 minutes. Garnish with watercress sprigs. Serve immediately

Serves 3–4

Mrs J. Mary · Bath

Fillet of Pork Pierre

450g (1lb) pork fillet
25g (1oz) flour
salt and pepper
1 onion, skinned and finely chopped
50g (2oz) English butter
150ml (¼ pint) dry white wine
pinch cayenne
freshly chopped parsley
2 slices of white bread, crusts removed, cut in triangles
150ml (5 fl oz) fresh single cream
225g (8oz) Leicester cheese, finely grated

1 Cut the pork into 2cm (¾ inch) cubes and coat with seasoned flour

2 Gently fry the onion and pork in 25g (1oz) butter for 5 minutes. Add the wine, cayenne and a little parsley. Simmer gently for 15 minutes

3 Melt the remaining butter and use to fry the bread triangles quickly until crisp and golden

4 Add the cream to the pork and 175g (6oz) cheese, season to taste. Heat until cheese has melted. Do not allow to boil

5 Turn into a warm serving dish, sprinkle on the remaining cheese. Brown under the grill

6 Serve immediately garnished with fresh parsley and bread triangles

Serves 4

Miss J. A. Wilson · Whitby

Left: Pork Fillet en Croûte. Right: Poussins with Stilton Cream Sauce

Ham en Croûte

900g (2lb) gammon joint
2 bay leaves
175g (6oz) plain flour
pinch of salt
100g (4oz) English butter
100g (4oz) English Cheshire cheese, grated
3 tablespoons water
2 tablespoons honey
1 egg, beaten
bunch of watercress, washed and trimmed

1 Soak the gammon for 12 hours. Drain, cover with water, add the bay leaves and bring to the boil. Simmer for 1 hour

2 Leave the gammon in the water and allow to go cold. Remove from the pan and cut off the skin and fat. Leave to cool

3 Place flour and salt in a bowl. Add the butter in pieces and rub into the flour until the mixture resembles fine breadcrumbs. Add the cheese

4 Add the water and mix to a dough. Knead lightly. Wrap in foil and chill for 1 hour

5 Spread honey over the joint. Roll out the pastry large enough to enclose the meat. Place the meat in the centre of the pastry and fold the edges over. Seal with a little egg, and place on a baking sheet with the join underneath. Glaze with beaten egg

6 Bake 200°C (400°F), mark 6, for 30 minutes until the pastry is risen and golden

7 Serve on a bed of watercress. This dish freezes well at the uncooked stage. Thaw for about 3 hours before cooking

Serves 4–6

Sue Stevens · Bradford

Chicken Stuffed with Blue Stilton in a Rich Port Sauce

4 boned chicken breasts
100g (4oz) Blue Stilton cheese
flour
50g (2oz) English butter
1 glass of port
100g (4oz) seedless grapes
300ml (10 fl oz) fresh double cream
salt and pepper
watercress sprigs, washed and trimmed

1 Skin the chicken breasts and place in a wet polythene bag and beat with a rolling pin, until flattened

2 Cream the cheese until soft, then divide into 4 portions and spread down the centre of each chicken breast

3 Roll up neatly and secure with a wooden cocktail stick. Toss in flour and chill in the refrigerator for 15 minutes

4 Melt the butter in a frying pan and gently fry the chicken for 5 minutes, then transfer to an ovenproof dish with any of the remaining butter

5 Bake 180°C (350°F), mark 4, for 25 to 30 minutes

6 Add the port to the frying pan and reduce by half. Stir in the grapes and fresh cream and simmer until thickened. Add seasoning to taste

7 Pour over the chicken and serve garnished with watercress

Serves 4

Mrs C. Hornsby · Edinburgh

Poussins with Stilton Cream Sauce

4 poussins
salt and pepper
100g (4oz) English butter
225g (8oz) mushrooms, sliced
4 tablespoons brandy
300ml (10 fl oz) fresh single cream
100g (4oz) Blue Stilton cheese
parsley sprigs

1 Wash the poussins and remove any remaining feathers. Season with salt and pepper and dot with 50g (2oz) butter

3 Cook the mushrooms in the remaining butter for 5 minutes. Season with salt and pepper to taste. Reduce the heat, add the brandy and marinate the mushrooms for 15 minutes

4 Increase the heat, stir in the fresh cream, heat stirring continuously until the sauce thickens. Crumble the Stilton into the sauce; stir until the cheese has melted

5 Pour half of the sauce over the cooked poussins and serve remaining sauce separately. Garnish with parsley. Serve immediately

Serves 4

Miss Lesley Quinn · London N1

Crown Derby

450ml (¾ pint) chicken stock
1 level tablespoon gelatine
4 eggs, hard-boiled
3 carrots, peeled and finely grated
100g (4oz) Derby cheese, grated
chopped chives
225ml (8 fl oz) fresh double cream, whipped

1 Place 3 tablespoons of the cold stock in a bowl and sprinkle in the gelatine. Stand the bowl over a saucepan of hot water and heat gently until dissolved. Leave to cool, but not set

2 Liquidise or sieve the eggs. Stir in the carrots, cheese and chives

3 Fold in the whipped cream and pour into an oiled brioche or similar mould. Chill in the refrigerator until set

4 Dip mould quickly into hot water, to loosen, and turn out carefully on to a serving plate

Serves 8

This dish also makes an impressive starter at a dinner party made in individual moulds

Dr S. J. G. Caldwell · Dundee

Special Cheesy Parsnips

900g (2lb) parsnips, peeled
3 tablespoons vegetable oil
75g (3oz) English butter
2 level tablespoons soft brown sugar
salt and freshly ground black pepper
300ml (10 fl oz) fresh single cream
450g (1lb) tomatoes, skinned, seeded and sliced
175g (6oz) Double Gloucester cheese, grated
4 tablespoons fresh white breadcrumbs

1 Cut away any hard central cores from the parsnips and slice thinly. Fry in oil for 4 minutes

2 Butter a 1·1 litre (2 pint) ovenproof casserole, using half of the butter. Place a layer of parsnips on the base, sprinkle with a little sugar, seasoning and pour over a little of the cream

3 Cover with a layer of tomatoes, add a little more cream and some cheese. Repeat these layers until all the ingredients have been used, finishing with a layer of cream and cheese

4 Sprinkle with breadcrumbs and add the remaining butter and cover

5 Bake 170°C (350°F), mark 3, for 50 to 60 minutes. Serve immediately

Serves 4–6

Mrs M. A. Williams · Plymouth

Rich Rice

1 green eating apple, cored and thinly sliced
1 red eating apple, cored and thinly sliced
juice of ½ lemon
150ml (5 fl oz) fresh double cream, whipped
200ml (7 fl oz) mayonnaise
1 level teaspoon curry powder
450g (1lb) English Cheddar cheese, cut into 1cm
  (½ inch) cubes
225g (8oz) green grapes
salt and freshly ground pepper
175g (6oz) long grain rice, cooked and drained
watercress sprigs

1 Toss the apple slices in lemon juice

2 Fold the whipped cream into the mayonnaise with the curry powder, cheese, grapes, apples, lemon juice and seasoning, to taste

3 Pile on top of the rice and serve garnished with watercress

Serves 8

Mrs M. H. Hicks · Bristol

Stilton Sweet and Savoury

175g (6oz) digestive biscuits, crushed
175g (6oz) soft brown sugar
75g (3oz) English butter, melted
4 cloves
700g (1 ½lb) cooking apples, peeled, cored and chopped
1 tablespoon demerara sugar
175g (6oz) Blue Stilton cheese, cut into cubes
1 tablespoon port
100ml (4 fl oz) fresh double cream
walnuts

1 Mix biscuits with 75g (3oz) of the sugar and the butter

2 Press on to the base and 4cm (1½ inches) up the sides of a 20cm (8 inch) loose-bottomed cake tin or spring form tin

3 Bake 180°C (350°F), mark 4, for 30 minutes. Cool, then chill in the refrigerator

4 Add the remaining soft brown sugar, cloves and a little water to the apple. Cook until tender, drain off juice and chill

5 Carefully remove biscuit base from tin, place on a serving dish. Fill with the apple mixture and sprinkle with demerara sugar

6 Place the Stilton in a saucepan and warm *very gently* until soft but *not* runny. Allow to cool, then gradually add the port and cream, whisking until smooth

7 Place in a piping bag fitted with a large star nozzle and pipe rosettes on top of the apple

8 Decorate with walnuts and chill

Serves 6–8

Mrs J. Fox · Ferndown

Carrot Ring with Cheese

450g (1lb) carrots, cooked and mashed
175g (6oz) English Cheddar cheese
50g (2oz) fresh white breadcrumbs
2 tablespoons minced onions
2 tablespoons melted butter
2 eggs, beaten
1 tablespoon plain flour
300ml (10 fl oz) fresh single cream
salt and freshly ground pepper
paprika

1 Mix all the ingredients together and place in a well buttered 1·1 litre (2 pint) ring mould

2 Place in a baking tin half filled with hot water.

3 Bake 180°C (350°F), mark 4, for 40 to 45 minutes, until set. Turn out on to a plate and fill with vegetables of your choice to accompany a meat dish or fill with creamed chicken to make a complete meal

Serves 6–8

Mrs K. Gilbert · Southampton

Left to right: Potted Cheese with Walnuts, Cheddar Cream, Cheese Mousse

Cheddar Cream

225g (8oz) mature English Cheddar cheese, grated
100g (4oz) English butter
2 tablespoons whisky liqueur
freshly ground black pepper
coarse oatmeal, toasted

1 Cream the cheese and butter together, gradually adding the whisky liqueur. Season to taste

2 Chill, then shape into a roll. Coat with oatmeal and serve with oatcakes or cheese biscuits and a 'nip' of whisky, for that special occasion

Serves 8

Mary E. Browning · Glasgow

Potted Cheese with Walnuts

75g (3oz) Blue Stilton cheese, crumbled
75g (3oz) English Cheddar cheese, grated
75g (3oz) English butter, softened
1 level teaspoon French mustard
1–2 tablespoons medium-dry sherry
50–75g (2–3oz) broken walnuts

1 Mix cheeses with the butter and mustard. Gradually stir in the sherry until a very firm paste is formed (the amount of sherry depends on the dryness of the cheese)

2 Stir in the walnuts and pack firmly into an earthenware pot or soufflé dish and cover. Serve with a variety of cheese biscuits

Serves 6–8

Mrs Diane Tidd · Epsom

Cheese Mousse

150ml (5 fl oz) fresh double cream, whipped
100g (4oz) mature English Cheddar cheese, finely grated
100g (4oz) Double Gloucester cheese, finely grated
25g (1oz) almonds, chopped
2 tablespoons water
15g (½oz) gelatine
2 egg whites, whisked
salt and freshly ground black pepper
1 level teaspoon made mustard
maraschino cherries
parsley sprigs

1 Carefully mix the whipped cream with the cheeses and almonds until well combined

2 Place the 2 tablespoons cold water in a bowl and sprinkle in the gelatine. Stand the bowl over a saucepan of hot water and heat gently until dissolved. Leave to cool a little

3 Fold the egg whites into the cheese mixture, add seasoning and mustard

4 Fold in the dissolved gelatine and pour into a 900ml (1½ pint) soufflé dish or a 450g (1lb) loaf tin and chill until set

5 Turn out and garnish with cherries and parsley

Serves 10–12

Mrs H. Clayfield · Wrexham

Stilton Sausage Balls

225g (8oz) sausagemeat
salt and freshly ground pepper
½ level teaspoon mixed herbs
100g (4oz) Blue Stilton cheese
1 egg, lightly beaten
100g (4oz) dry white breadcrumbs
vegetable oil for deep frying
1 bunch watercress, trimmed and washed (optional)

1 Mix the sausagemeat with plenty of seasoning and the herbs until thoroughly combined, then divide into 12 equal portions. Cut the cheese into 12 small cubes

2 Flatten one portion of sausagemeat in the palm of your hand. Place a cube of cheese in the middle, then knead the sausagemeat around the cheese to enclose it completely and form a neat ball. Repeat until all the sausagemeat and cheese are used

3 Dip the savouries first in the beaten egg, then in the breadcrumbs, making sure they are evenly and thoroughly coated with crumbs

4 Heat the oil for deep frying to 180°C (350°F). Cook the Stilton sausage balls in the oil until golden brown, then drain on absorbent kitchen paper

5 Serve hot, in a napkin-lined basket, or allow to cool and arrange on a bed of watercress

Makes 12

Sally Forster · Brill

Pork and Cheese Eggs

700g (1½lb) minced pork
1 small onion, skinned and finely chopped
1 apple, peeled, cored and grated
1 level teaspoon dried sage
salt and pepper
1 egg yolk
1 egg, beaten
golden breadcrumbs
12 × 2cm (¾ inch) cubes of English Cheddar cheese
oil, to fry
celery leaves

1 Mix pork, onion, apple, sage, seasoning and egg yolk. Divide into 12 portions and mould each into an egg shape using floured hands. Chill for 30 minutes

2 Brush with egg and coat with breadcrumbs. Press a cube of cheese into each one so that the surface of the cheese shows through the breadcrumbs

3 Deep fry for 10 to 15 minutes until crisp golden brown and cooked right through

4 Garnish with celery leaves and serve with spicy tomato sauce

Serves 6

Mrs D. Bell · Eastleigh

Devilled Eclairs

60g (2½oz) plain flour
pinch of salt
150ml (¼ pint) water
75g (3oz) English butter
2 eggs, beaten
175g (6oz) English Cheddar cheese, grated
2 tablespoons tomato ketchup
1 tablespoon Worcestershire sauce
1 level tablespoon made mustard
yeast extract
chopped parsley

1 To make the choux pastry, sift the flour and salt together twice

2 Place the water and 50g (2oz) of butter in a saucepan and heat until the liquid boils

3 Remove the pan from the heat and tip in all the flour. Beat briskly with a wooden spoon until the mixture leaves the sides of the pan. Allow to cool

4 Gradually beat in the eggs, and 50g (2oz) cheese, beating well between each addition. The mixture should be glossy and firm enough to stand in soft peaks

5 Pipe or spoon the mixture on to a buttered baking sheet

6 Bake 220°C (425°F), mark 7, for 15 to 20 minutes. Slit the sides and leave in the oven for 5 minutes. Cool on a wire rack

7 To make the filling, soften the remaining butter in a bowl then blend in the tomato ketchup, Worcestershire sauce and mustard. Fill the éclairs with the cheese mixture

8 Spread each éclair with a little yeast extract and dip into chopped parsley

Makes 36 small éclairs

E. Sowden · Leigh-on-Sea

A tasty and interesting addition to a cheeseboard can be made from mixing equal quantities of full fat soft cheese and grated English cheese (any variety).
Mould the cheese mixture into a sausage shape and roll in crushed cornflakes or ground nuts; chill in the refrigerator before serving

Mrs Dianne Clark · Sutton-upon-Derwent

When preparing a cheeseboard, take 2 or 3 apples, preferably red skinned, and cut out thin wedges all round the fruit. Then cut pieces of cheese roughly the same size as the wedges and fill the gaps with the cheese. This makes a colourful and appetising addition to the cheeseboard for any guest who likes fruit with their cheese

Mrs H. Williams · Sawbridge

Cheese Dates

227-g (8-oz) box fine, smooth dates
225g (8oz) English Cheddar cheese, finely grated
½ level teaspoon made mustard
8 drops of Angostura bitters
about 50g (2oz) blanched almonds, toasted

1 Split the dates and remove the stones

2 Beat the cheese, mustard and Angostura bitters together into a smooth paste. Count the dates and divide the cheese mixture into a similar number of equal portions. Form the portions of cheese into small rolls

3 Stuff each of the dates with a roll of cheese and press an almond on top

4 Place the dates in small paper sweet cases and serve

Makes about 30

Also delicious served at a cheese and wine party

Mrs V. E. Swann · Corsham

Stilton Caribbean Savouries

225g (8oz) White Stilton cheese, grated
50g (2oz) sultanas
1 banana, finely chopped
50g (2oz) fresh brown breadcrumbs
1 dessert apple, peeled and grated
1 level teaspoon curry powder
cocktail sticks

1 Mix the cheese with the sultanas and banana. Add the breadcrumbs, apple and curry powder to taste, then use a wooden spoon to mix all the ingredients together thoroughly

2 Knead small portions of the mixture into balls about the size of a walnut. Chill slightly, then serve on cocktail sticks

Makes 24

D. F. Wheeler · Swaffham

Top left: Devilled Eclairs. Top right: Stilton Caribbean Savouries
Bottom left: Cheese Dates. Bottom Right: Cheese Oatcakes

Desserts and Puddings

It is traditional to serve Apple Pie and Wensleydale cheese in Yorkshire but it is more usual to associate soft cheeses with puddings, such as cheesecake. The ingenious blending of cheese in these dishes will keep your friends guessing and they are bound to want the recipe from you.

Raspberry and Orange Cheese Flan

175g (6oz) plain flour
pinch of salt
grated rind of 1 orange
175g (6oz) caster sugar
90g (3½oz) English butter
juice of 1 medium and 2 large oranges
225g (8oz) fresh or just thawed frozen raspberries
75g (3oz) Lancashire cheese, crumbled or grated
3 eggs, beaten
100ml (4 fl oz) fresh double cream, whipped

1 Place the flour, salt, orange rind and 50g (2oz) of the sugar in a bowl. Add the butter in pieces and rub into the flour until the mixture resembles fine breadcrumbs. Add 1 tablespoon of the orange juice and mix into a dough. Chill

2 Roll out on a lightly floured work top and line a 23cm (9 inch) flan ring

3 Reserve a few raspberries for decoration and place the remaining fruit in the flan case and sprinkle the cheese on top

4 Beat remaining sugar with the eggs and remaining orange juice. Pour into the flan case

5 Bake 190°C (375°F), mark 5, for 30 to 35 minutes. Allow to cool

6 Decorate with reserved raspberries. Serve with whipped cream

Serves 4–6

Barbara Briggs · Preston

Lemon Wensleydale Tart

100g (4oz) shortcrust pastry made with 100g (4oz) plain
  flour (page 116)
1 teaspoon lemon rind, finely grated
100g (4oz) Wensleydale cheese, finely grated
3 tablespoons homemade lemon curd
1 egg
50g (2oz) sultanas
juice of 1 small lemon

1 Make up half quantity shortcrust pastry (page 116),
and add lemon rind

2 Knead lightly and roll out on a floured work top and
line a 18cm (7 inch) flan dish. Reserve any left over
pastry

3 Beat together cheese, lemon curd, egg, sultanas and
lemon juice and place in the flan case

4 Decorate with twists of pastry

5 Bake 200°C (400°F), mark 6, for 25 minutes, until set.
Serve hot or cold with fresh cream

Serves 4

Mrs S. Caudwell · Worksop

Spiced Apple Cheese Flan

175g (6oz) shortcrust pastry made with 175g (6oz) plain
  flour (page 116)
100g (4oz) English Cheddar cheese, grated
2 eggs, beaten
450g (1lb) cooking apples, peeled, cored and chopped
50g (2oz) caster sugar
pinch of ground cinnamon

1 Make up three-quarters quantity shortcrust pastry
(page 116)

2 Knead lightly and roll out on a lightly floured work top
and line a 20·5cm (8 inch) flan ring. Prick the base

3 Bake 'blind' 200°C (400°F), mark 6, for 10 to 15
minutes

4 Mix the cheese and eggs and pour into the flan case

5 Toss apples in sugar and cinnamon and place in flan
case

6 Bake 180°C (350°F), mark 4, for 40 to 50 minutes.
Serve hot or cold

Serves 4–6

Christine Young · Southampton

Left to right: Raspberry and Orange Cheese Flan, Lemon
Wensleydale Tart, Spiced Apple Cheese Flan

Cheese and Fruit Brûlée

Cheese and Fruit Brûlée

100g (4oz) grapes, pips removed
225g (8oz) eating apples, peeled, cored and chopped
3 tablespoons lemon juice
50g (2oz) seedless raisins
1 banana, peeled and sliced
25g (1oz) Brazil nuts, chopped
100g (4oz) Wensleydale cheese, coarsley grated
450ml (15 fl oz) fresh double cream, whipped
100–175g (4–6oz) demerara sugar

1 Mix grapes, apples, lemon juice, raisins, banana, nuts and cheese together. Place in an ovenproof serving dish

2 Spread the whipped cream on top and chill for 1 to 2 hours

3 Cover generously with sugar and place under a very hot grill until the sugar caramelises. Serve immediately

Serves 4–6

S. Clark · Leigh-on-Sea

Ginger Cheesecake

100g (4oz) English butter
75g (3oz) caster sugar
3 tablespoons black treacle
175g (6oz) ginger biscuits, crushed
1 teaspoon lemon juice
50g (2oz) icing sugar
50g (2oz) sultanas
75g (3oz) unsalted peanuts, roasted and crushed
150g (5oz) English Cheddar cheese, finely grated
75ml (3 fl oz) fresh whipping cream, whipped

1 Melt the butter, sugar and treacle and stir in the biscuit crumbs

2 Press on to the base of a 18cm (7 inch) tin and leave to set

3 Fold the lemon juice, sugar, sultanas, nuts and cheese into the whipped cream. Spread over the biscuit base and chill until set

Serves 4

Jenny A. Moon · Glasgow

Hawaiian Cheese Dessert

397-g (13¼-oz) can crushed pineapple
2 tablespoons cornflour
2 tablespoons water
100g (4oz) English Cheshire cheese, grated
175g (6oz) granulated sugar
50g (2oz) English butter
50g (2oz) self-raising flour
2 eggs
300ml (½ pint) milk
1 teaspoon vanilla essence

1 Heat the pineapple in a saucepan over a gentle heat

2 Blend cornflour with the cold water and stir into the pineapple. Heat, stirring continuously, until the sauce thickens and boils. Spread evenly over the base of a 23cm (9 inch) pie dish and cool

3 Mix together the cheese, sugar and butter. Add the flour and blend well

4 Add the eggs, one at a time, beating well

5 Gradually stir in the milk and essence until a smooth batter is obtained. Pour over the pineapple

6 Bake 230°C (450°F), mark 8, for 10 minutes, then reduce temperature to 180°C (350°F), mark 4, for a further 30 minutes. Serve hot or cold

Serves 6

S. J. Brunt · Newark

Coconut Lemon Cheesecake

175g (6oz) shortcrust pastry made with 175g (6oz) plain flour (page 116)
4 tablespoons red jam
75g (3oz) Wensleydale cheese, finely grated
75g (3oz) caster sugar
2 eggs
grated rind and juice of 1 lemon
150g (5oz) desiccated coconut

1 Make up three-quarters quantity shortcrust pastry (page 116)

2 Knead lightly and roll out on a floured work top and line a 18cm (7 inch) pie dish

3 Spread the base with jam

4 Cream the cheese with the sugar and beat in the eggs

5 Stir in the lemon rind and juice with the coconut and spread on top of the jam

6 Bake 180°C (350°F), mark 4, for 30 to 40 minutes, until golden brown. Serve hot with fresh cream

Serves 4

Mrs J. B. Gibson-Leitch · Hinckley

Cheese, Apple and Sultana Pudding

225g (8oz) wholemeal flour
2 level teaspoons baking powder
½ teaspoon salt
50g (2oz) English butter
75g (3oz) demerara sugar
75g (3oz) English Cheshire cheese, grated
1 large apple, peeled, cored and grated
50g (2oz) sultanas
1 egg
142g (5oz) natural yogurt
4–5 tablespoons milk

1 Place the flour, baking powder and salt into a bowl. Add the butter in pieces and rub into the flour until the mixture resembles fine breadcrumbs

2 Stir in the sugar, cheese, apple and sultanas and mix into a soft dough with the egg, yogurt and milk. Place in a well buttered 900ml (1½ pint) pudding basin, and cover

3 Steam for 1½ hours. Turn out and serve immediately. Serve with fresh cream

Serves 4–6

Mrs Angela Mottram · Axbridge

Welsh William's Flan

175g (6oz) shortcrust pastry made with 175g (6oz) plain flour (page 116)
50g (2oz) English butter
50g (2oz) demerara sugar
2 eggs
100g (4oz) Caerphilly cheese, finely grated
50g (2oz) ground almonds
a few drops of almond essence (optional)
822-g (1lb 13-oz) can pear halves, drained

1 Make up three-quarters quantity shortcrust pastry (page 116)

2 Knead lightly and roll out on a lightly floured board and line a 23cm (9 inch) flan ring

3 Cream the butter and sugar together. Beat in the eggs, cheese, ground almonds and almond essence if used

4 Spread this mixture in the base of the flan case and arrange the pear halves on top

5 Bake at 200°C (400°F), mark 6, for 20 minutes and then reduce heat to 170°C (325°F), mark 3, for a further 20 minutes or until golden brown and firm to the touch. Cool in the flan ring

Serves 8

Mrs M. A. Constable · Blacon

Russian Cherry Cake

425-g (15-oz) can pitted black cherries
135-g (4¾-oz) packet blackcurrant jelly
18–20 sponge finger or lanque de chat biscuits
225g (8oz) English Cheddar cheese, finely grated
450ml (15 fl oz) fresh double cream, whipped

1 Drain the juice from the cherries and make up to 300ml (½ pint) with boiling water. Pour over the jelly in a bowl and stir until dissolved

2 Pour 0·5cm (¼ inch) layer of jelly into the base of a 18cm (7 inch) cake tin, and allow to set

3 Decorate the jelly base with a few of the cherries

4 Carefully place the biscuits around the edge of the tin with the curved sides against the sides of the tin

5 Fold the cheese into 300ml (½ pint) of the whipped cream with the remaining cherries. Pour into the cake tin and allow to set

6 Trim the biscuits to the level of the mixture. Dip the base of the tin in hot water for a few seconds, then turn out on to a serving plate. Decorate with rosettes of the remaining whipped cream

Serves 6–8

Mrs H. Grant · Kilmarnock

Ennid Cake

100g (4oz) English butter
100g (4oz) soft brown sugar
2 eggs
100g (4oz) Caerphilly cheese, grated
75g (3oz) mincemeat
25g (1oz) candied peel
200g (7oz) self-raising flour
a few flaked almonds

1 Cream the butter and sugar together until light and fluffy

2 Beat in the eggs one at a time

3 Stir in the cheese, mincemeat and peel, and fold in the flour

4 Place the mixture in a well buttered and lightly floured 18cm (7 inch) cake tin. Sprinkle almonds on top

5 Bake 190°C (375°F), mark 5, for 10 minutes, then reduce temperature to 170°C (325°F), mark 3, for a further hour. Allow to cool in the tin. Ideal served with cheese

Serves 6–8

Ellsie Russell · Fleet

Russian Cherry Cake

Cheshire Cheesecake

Cheshire Cheesecake

225g (8oz) digestive biscuits, crushed
100g (4oz) English butter, melted
175g (6oz) caster sugar
225g (8oz) English Cheshire cheese, finely grated
2 level teaspoons custard powder
2 eggs, beaten
150ml (5 fl oz) fresh whipping cream
1 tablespoon lemon juice
½ teaspoon vanilla essence
300ml (10 fl oz) soured cream
4 strawberries
1 kiwi fruit

1 Mix biscuits with butter and stir in 1 tablespoon caster sugar. Press on to base and sides of a 20·5cm (8 inch) loose-bottomed springform tin

2 Bake 170°C (325°F), mark 3, for 5 minutes

3 Place cheese, 100g (4oz) of the sugar and custard powder in a basin and beat well. Add eggs, whipping cream and lemon juice, beat thoroughly. Pour into the biscuit base

4 Bake 170°C (325°F), mark 3, for 35 to 40 minutes until set. Remove from the oven and cool for 15 minutes

5 Beat remaining sugar and vanilla essence with soured cream and pour over the cheesecake

6 Bake 220°C (425°F), mark 7, for 15 minutes. Remove from the oven, cool then chill. Decorate with strawberry halves and kiwi fruit slices

Serves 6–8

S. Giles · Ruddington

Wensleydale Apple Cake

225g (8oz) self-raising flour
100g (4oz) caster sugar
½ teaspoon salt
175g (6oz) English butter
1 egg, beaten
50ml (2 fl oz) milk
3 medium apples, peeled, cored and sliced
100g (4oz) Wensleydale cheese, grated
½ level teaspoon ground cinnamon
lemon juice
golden syrup, optional

1 Place flour, 50g (2oz) of the sugar and salt into a bowl. Add 100g (4oz) butter in pieces and rub into the flour until the mixture resembles fine breadcrumbs

2 Add the egg and milk and mix into a soft dough. Spread into a well buttered 20·5cm (8 inch) cake tin

3 Arrange half the apple slices on top and sprinkle with cheese

4 Add the remaining apples and sprinkle remaining sugar and cinnamon on top. Dot with remaining butter and lemon juice

5 Bake 200°C (400°F), mark 6, for 45 minutes. Pour a little melted syrup over the cake, if liked

Serves 6–8

M. Osher · West Withington

Cheese and Mandarin Flan

175g (6oz) shortcrust pastry made with 175g (6oz) plain flour (page 116)
2 eggs yolks
50g (2oz) caster sugar
15g (½oz) cornflour
150ml (¼ pint) milk
100g (4oz) English Cheshire cheese, finely grated
200ml (7 fl oz) fresh double cream, whipped
mandarin oranges, drained if canned

1 Make up three-quarters quantity shortcrust pastry (page 116)

2 Knead lightly and roll out on a floured work top and line a 20·5cm (8 inch) flan case. Prick the base

3 Bake 'blind' 200°C (400°F), mark 6, for 10 to 15 minutes then reduce temperature to 180°C (350°F), mark 4, for a further 15 minutes

4 Beat egg yolks and sugar until well mixed. Blend cornflour with a little of the milk and add to the egg mixture

5 Heat remaining milk, but do not allow to boil and pour into the egg mixture. Bring to the boil, stirring continuously

6 Stir in the cheese, remove from the heat and whisk well. Allow to cool

7 Fold three-quarters of the whipped cream into the cooled mixture and pour into the pastry case

8 Decorate with rosettes of remaining whipped cream and mandarin oranges. Serve chilled

Serves 4–6

Mrs J. Howard · Framlingham

Golden Apricot Flan

175g (6oz) shortcrust pastry made with 175g (6oz) plain flour (page 116)
100g (4oz) dried apricots, soaked overnight
100g (4oz) Double Gloucester or Leicester cheese, grated
50g (2oz) blanched almonds or hazelnuts, chopped
25–50g (1–2oz) demerara sugar

1 Make up three-quarters quantity shortcrust pastry (page 116)

2 Knead lightly and roll out on a floured work top and line a 18cm (7 inch) flan ring

3 Drain the apricots and chop. Spread on the base of the flan. Sprinkle the cheese, nuts and sugar on top

4 Bake 200°C (400°F), mark 6, for 20 to 25 minutes. Serve hot or cold

Serves 4

Mrs R. Miners · Marazion

Berried Treasure Pie

225g (8oz) shortcrust pastry made with 225g (8oz) plain flour (page 116)
700g (1½lb) blackberries, washed
75g (3oz) sugar
75g (3oz) Caerphilly cheese, grated
a little milk

1 Make the shortcrust pastry (page 116). Knead lightly on a lightly-floured work top then roll out two-thirds and use to line a 23cm (9 inch) pie plate

2 Fill with the blackberries and sprinkle 50g (2oz) of the sugar over them. Top with the cheese

3 Roll out the remaining pastry large enough to cover the pie. Dampen the edge of the pastry base and lift the pastry cover over the filling

4 Press down the edges and seal them together by gently knocking up with the blunt knife edge between your thumb and forefinger to give a neat edge

5 Brush the top of the pie with a little milk, then sprinkle the remaining sugar over. Stand the pie on a baking sheet

6 Bake in the oven at 220°C (425°F), mark 7, for 15 minutes, then reduce the temperature to 180°C (350°F), mark 4, and continue to cook for a further 15 minutes, until golden brown. Serve hot or warm

Serves 6

Mrs Paul O'Keeffe · Heswall

Cheshire and Apricot Soufflé

25g (1oz) English butter
15g (½oz) plain flour
150ml (¼ pint) milk
3 eggs, separated
25g (1oz) caster sugar
100g (4oz) English Cheshire cheese, grated
410-g (14½-oz) can apricots, drained and chopped
1 tablespoon redcurrant jelly
grated nutmeg

1 Place the butter, flour and milk in a saucepan, heat, stirring continuously until the sauce thickens, boils and is smooth. Cook for 1 minute

2 Cool slightly and beat in the egg yolks, sugar, cheese, apricots and redcurrant jelly

3 Whisk the egg whites until standing in stiff peaks, then fold into the sauce

4 Pour into a well buttered 1 litre (2 pint) soufflé dish and sprinkle with grated nutmeg

5 Bake 190°C (375°F), mark 5, for 20 to 30 minutes. Serve immediately

Serves 4

Mrs Mary Solway · Plymouth

Granny's Pudding

700g (1½lb) cooking apples, cooked and puréed
175g (6oz) caster sugar
2 eggs, separated
100g (4oz) Double Gloucester cheese, finely grated
25g (1oz) flaked almonds

1 Place the puréed apples in 20·5cm (8 inch) ovenproof flan dish

2 Sprinkle 25g (1oz) of the sugar on top

3 Whisk egg yolks with 25g (1oz) of the sugar until creamy and stir in the cheese. Spread over the apple purée and sprinkle with almonds

4 Whisk the egg whites until standing in stiff peaks, then fold in remaining sugar. Place in a piping bag, fitted with a star nozzle, and pipe over the cheese mixture, making sure it is completely covered

5 Bake 180°C (350°F), mark 4, for 15 minutes. Serve hot

Serves 6

Mrs Deidre Cobb · Swithland

Left: Granny's Pudding. Right: Tangy Apple Pie

Tangy Apple Pie

225g (8oz) plain flour
pinch of salt
100g (4oz) English butter
2 level teaspoons caster sugar
1 tablespoon custard powder
3–4 tablespoons milk
450g (1lb) Bramley cooking apples, peeled, cored and thinly sliced
25g (1oz) sultanas
75g (3oz) Lancashire or Wensleydale cheese, grated
50g (2oz) soft brown sugar
1 tablespoon natural yogurt
milk or beaten egg

1 Place flour and salt into a bowl. Add the butter in pieces and rub into the flour until the mixture resembles fine breadcrumbs

2 Stir in the sugar and custard powder and add sufficient milk to make a soft dough. Allow to rest in the refrigerator

3 Roll out pastry on a lightly floured work top and use half to line 20·5cm (8 inch) pie dish

4 Mix apples, sultanas, grated cheese, sugar and yogurt together, and place in the pie dish

5 Use remaining pastry to make a lid for the pie. Seal and flute the edges and make a vent in the top. Brush with milk or egg

6 Bake 200°C (400°F), mark 6, for 30 minutes. Serve hot with fresh cream

Serves 6

Plum Quiche

Plum Quiche

225g (8oz) shortcrust pastry made with 225g (8oz) plain
flour (page 116)
700g (1½lb) English plums, halved and stoned
100g (4oz) caster sugar
grated nutmeg
2 eggs
150ml (5 fl oz) fresh single cream
100g (4oz) Wensleydale cheese, grated

1 Make up shortcrust pastry (page 116)

2 Knead lightly and roll out on a floured work top and
line a 33 × 23cm (13 × 9 inch) Swiss roll tin

3 Arrange plums, cut side uppermost, on the pastry and
sprinkle with 50g (2oz) of the sugar and grated nutmeg
to taste

4 Bake 200°C (400°F), mark 6, for 15 minutes

5 Beat eggs with fresh cream, cheese and remaining
sugar and pour over the plums. Return to the oven
reduced to 180°C (350°F), mark 4, for a further 30
minutes. Serve cold

Serves 8

Mrs Jenny Carpenter · Sheffield

Cheese and Treacle Tart

175g (6oz) shortcrust pastry made with 175g (6oz) plain
    flour (page 116)
225g (8oz) English Cheddar cheese, grated
6 tablespoons golden syrup, warmed
2 teaspoons lemon juice
25g (1oz) fresh white breadcrumbs
2 eggs
150ml (¼ pint) milk

1 Make up three-quarters quantity shortcrust pastry
(page 116)

2 Knead lightly and roll out on a floured work top and
line a 20·5cm (8 inch) flan dish, reserving any left over
pastry

3 Sprinkle half of the cheese on the base of the flan and
pour over the warmed syrup

4 Sprinkle with lemon juice and cover with the remaining
cheese and breadcrumbs

5 Beat eggs and milk together and pour into the flan

6 Cut any remaining pastry into thin strips and arrange in
a lattice design over the flan

7 Bake 200°C (400°F), mark 6, for 30 to 35 minutes. Serve
hot or cold with fresh cream

Serves 4–6

Mrs Dorothy Walsh · Preston

Cheddar Apple Flan

225g (8oz) shortcrust pastry made with 225g (8oz) plain
    flour (page 116)
450g (1lb) cooking apples, peeled, cored and sliced
3 tablespoons undiluted orange squash
225g (8oz) granulated sugar
50g (2oz) English butter
2 eggs, beaten
75g (3oz) English Cheddar cheese, grated
125g (5 fl oz) soured cream

1 Make up shortcrust pastry (page 116)

2 Knead lightly and roll out on a floured work top and
line a 23cm (9 inch) flan ring

3 Cook the apples in the orange squash until soft.
Liquidise or sieve and place in a double saucepan or a
bowl over a pan of hot water

4 Add the sugar and the butter and stir over
a gentle heat until the sugar has dissolved

5 Add the eggs and continue to stir until the mixture
thickens. Remove from the heat

6 Stir in the cheese until melted, then allow to cool

7 Fill the flan with the apple curd mixture, reserving a
little for decoration

8 Bake 200°C (400°F), mark 6, for 30 minutes

9 Carefully spread the soured cream over the top and
bake for a further 10 minutes. Cool, then refrigerate

10 Just before serving spread the reserved apple curd
around the edge of the flan

Serves 6

Mrs P. L. Kearsey · Southend on Sea

Derby Peach Flan

175g (6oz) shortcrust pastry made with 175g (6oz) plain
    flour (page 116)
2 ripe fresh or canned peaches, drained
50g (2oz) English butter
50g (2oz) caster sugar
1 egg, beaten
100g (4oz) Derby cheese, finely grated
3 tablespoons fresh single cream
grated rind of 1 lemon

1 Make up three-quarters quantity shortcrust pastry
(page 116)

2 Knead lightly and roll out on a floured work top and
line a 20·5cm (8 inch) flan ring

3 Skin peaches if using fresh and slice. Arrange in the
pastry case

4 Cream the butter and sugar until light and fluffy

5 Beat in the egg, cheese, fresh cream and lemon rind,
and mix well together. Spread over the peaches

6 Bake 190°C (375°F), mark 5, for 35 minutes. Serve
cold

Serves 4– 6

Mr E. Liquorish · Birstall

Make mince pies in the normal way but do not
sprinkle them with sugar when cooked.
Before serving lift the lids and place a slice or a
little grated Wensleydale cheese over the
mincemeat. Replace the lids and place in the oven
190°C (375°F), mark 5, for 10–15 minutes

Mrs M. Morris · Stoke-on-Trent

Sweet 'n' Savoury Slices

215-g (7½-oz) packet frozen puff pastry, thawed
175g (6oz) English Cheddar cheese, grated
100g (4oz) cranberry sauce
175g (6oz) mixed nuts, chopped
pinch of salt
50g (2oz) light brown sugar
pinch of ground cinnamon

1 Roll out pastry on a lightly floured work top. Sprinkle one-quarter of the cheese over half of the pastry. Fold over and re-roll. Repeat three more times. Allow to rest in refrigerator for 30 minutes

2 Roll out into an oblong 40 × 20·5cm (16 × 8 inches) and cut in half, making 2 × 20·5cm (8 inch) squares

3 Mix remaining ingredients together. Place one piece of pastry on a damp baking sheet and spread filling over. Cover with remaining pastry and press edges together

4 Bake 200°C (400°F), mark 6, for 20 minutes. Cut into 9 slices and dredge with icing sugar

Makes 6–12 slices

Mrs P. Lanton · Walsall

Left to right: Sweet 'n' Savoury Slices, Walnut and Cheese Scone, Crunchy Cheese Squares, Fruity Cheese Turnover

Walnut and Cheese Scone

175g (6oz) plain flour
175g (6oz) wholemeal flour
1 level teaspoon ground cinnamon
½ teaspoon salt
175g (6oz) English butter
25—50g (1–2oz) soft brown sugar
75g (3oz) English Cheshire cheese, grated
75g (3oz) low fat soft (curd) cheese
300ml (½ pint) milk, approximately
225g (8oz) walnuts, finely chopped
75g (3oz) dates, finely chopped
175ml (6 fl oz) soured cream
100g (4oz) clear honey

1 Place the plain and wholemeal flours, spice and salt into a bowl

2 Add the butter in pieces and rub in until the mixture resembles fine breadcrumbs

3 Add the sugar, cheeses and sufficient milk to make a stiff dough. Spread evenly in a well buttered 33 × 23cm (13 × 9 inch) Swiss roll tin

4 Mix the nuts, dates, soured cream and honey together and spread over the top

5 Bake 180°C (350°F), mark 4, for 1 hour. Serve hot with fresh cream

Makes 24 triangles

Mrs A. F. Mundy · Ventnor

Crunchy Cheese Squares

350g (12oz) plain flour
¼ teaspoon salt
175g (6oz) English butter
2 eggs, lightly beaten
2 tablespoons milk
225g (8oz) English Cheddar cheese, grated
1 egg, beaten
2 egg yolks
1 teaspoon lemon juice
100g (4oz) caster sugar
75g (3oz) currants
¼ teaspoon vanilla essence

1 Place the flour and salt into a bowl. Add the butter in pieces and rub into the flour until the mixture resembles fine breadcrumbs

2 Add the 2 lightly beaten eggs and milk and mix into a dough. Knead lightly and chill in the refrigerator for 30 minutes

3 Mix remaining ingredients together to make a filling

4 Roll out half the dough and line a 18 × 27·5cm (7 × 11 inch) rectangular tin

5 Spoon filling on to the pastry and spread evenly. Roll out remaining pastry and cover the filling, pressing the edges firmly together. Make a small air vent in the centre of the pastry and brush with milk

6 Bake 200°C (400°F), mark 6, for 25 to 30 minutes. Allow to cool, dredge with icing sugar and cut into squares

Serves 8

Miss Nadine Andrew · Sydenham

Fruity Cheese Turnover

215-g (7½-oz) packet frozen puff pastry, thawed
4–5 tablespoons mincemeat
450g (1lb) apples, peeled, cored and grated
75g (3oz) Wensleydale cheese
beaten egg white
caster sugar

1 Roll out pastry on a floured work top into a 30·5cm (12 inch) square

2 Spread mincemeat over half of the pastry

3 Mix apple and cheese together and spread on top of the mincemeat. Fold the other half of pastry over, sealing the edges well. Brush with beaten egg white and dredge with caster sugar

4 Bake 200°C (400°F), mark 6, for 20 to 25 minutes. Serve hot with fresh cream

Serves 6–8

Mrs G. E. Barratt · Worksop

Cheese and Wine

The simplest of impromptu parties can be a success with a range of English cheeses and crusty bread. But with a little planning and time, dips and dunks, bits on sticks, tartlets and savouries will give an impressive yet economical party.

Asparagus Cheese Toasties

20 medium-thick slices of white bread, with crusts removed
100g (4oz) English Cheddar cheese, grated
dash of Worcestershire sauce
paprika
½ level teaspoon made mustard (optional)
2 tablespoons milk
25g (1oz) English butter
298-g (10 ½ -oz) can asparagus spears, drained
2 tablespoons melted English butter
bunch of chives

1 Use a rolling pin to roll each slice of bread out thinly. Cover the slices with a damp cloth while preparing the filling

2 Mix the cheese with the Worcestershire sauce, paprika and mustard (if used)

3 Heat the milk and the 25g (1oz) butter together over gentle heat until the butter melts but do not boil. Pour this milk and butter into the cheese mixture and beat thoroughly until smooth

4 Spread some of the cheese mixture over each slice of bread. Place an asparagus spear on top of each slice and roll up tightly, dampening the edges of the bread to seal if necessary. Secure the rolls with wooden cocktail sticks

5 Place the rolls on a buttered baking sheet, brush the melted butter over the tops and bake in the oven at 220°C (425°F), mark 7, for about 10–15 minutes or until golden brown. Cool on a wire rack

6 Meanwhile, place the chives in a dish and cover with boiling water, leave to stand for 1 minute, then drain thoroughly

7 Garnish the toasties by first removing the cocktail sticks, then tie a strand of blanched chive around each

Serves 20

Miss Cecily L. Lake · St Albans

Wensleydale Toppers

75g (3oz) plain flour
25g (1oz) porridge oats
50g (2oz) English butter
100g (4oz) English Cheddar cheese, grated
1 egg yolk
100g (4oz) Wensleydale cheese, crumbled
¼ cucumber, peeled, finely chopped and drained
2–4 tablespoons soured cream
salt and freshly ground pepper
50g (2oz) peeled prawns (optional)
cayenne

1 Mix together the flour and oats, then rub in the butter until the mixture resembles fine breadcrumbs. Stir in the Cheddar cheese and egg yolk to form a firm dough

2 Roll out on a lightly floured work top to about 0·25cm (⅛ inch) thick. Cut out 5cm (2 inch) circles using a plain biscuit cutter, then place them slightly apart on buttered baking sheets

3 Bake in the oven at 200°C (400°F), mark 6, for 10–15 minutes. Cool on a wire rack

4 Meanwhile, mix the Wensleydale cheese with the cucumber and soured cream. Add seasoning to taste

5 Top each biscuit with a little of the cheese and cucumber mixture and garnish with a peeled prawn, if liked. Sprinkle with a little cayenne

Makes 30

Mrs J. Davie · Nottingham

Skippers

225g (8oz) Leicester cheese, finely grated
225g (8oz) kipper fillets, boned and poached
2 teaspoons chopped chives
2 tablespoons fresh single cream
50g (2oz) fresh white breadcrumbs
salt and freshly ground pepper
1 egg, beaten
100g (4oz) dry white breadcrumbs
vegetable oil for deep frying
cocktail sticks

1 Mash the cheese and kippers together with a fork. Add the chives, fresh cream and fresh breadcrumbs, then season to taste and mix thoroughly

2 Form the mixture into balls about the size of a walnut and dip each in beaten egg, then coat in dry breadcrumbs

3 Heat the oil for deep frying to 180°C (350°F). Fry the skippers, a few at a time, until golden brown. Drain on absorbent kitchen paper

4 Serve on cocktail sticks, either hot or cold. Remember to use wooden cocktail sticks if the skippers are hot

Makes 20

Mrs H. P. Ellis · Blackpool

Left: Asparagus Cheese Toasties. Right: Wensleydale Toppers

Cheddar Cheese and Celery Dip

50g (2oz) English butter
225g (8oz) English Cheddar cheese, finely grated
2 level teaspoons made mustard
100g (4oz) celery, finely chopped
142ml (5 fl oz) fresh single cream
salt and pepper
25g (1oz) salted peanuts, chopped

1 Beat butter until creamy. Stir in cheese, mustard and celery

2 Gradually beat in the fresh cream and season to taste

3 Serve sprinkled with peanuts

Serves 6–8

Blue Stilton and Avocado Dip

100g (4oz) Blue Stilton cheese
150ml (5 fl oz) soured cream
50g (2oz) walnuts, finely chopped
1 ripe avocado
1 tablespoon lemon juice
freshly ground pepper

1 Crumble the cheese, then mash it with a fork. Stir in the soured cream and walnuts

2 Halve the avocado, remove stone and scoop all the flesh out of the skin. Mash the flesh with the lemon juice, then add to the cheese mixture. Mix well and season to taste with pepper

3 Lightly chill the dip for about 30 minutes in a covered container before serving. Do not make up the mixture more than an hour in advance as the avocado may discolour with prolonged standing

4 Serve the dip with a selection of prepared, crisp raw vegetables – for example, carrots, cauliflower and celery – and small savoury biscuits or crisps

Serves 4–6

Mrs June Nicholls · Wilmslow

Combine equal quantities of Blue Stilton cheese and lightly whipped fresh double cream. Serve with hot seafood, such as scampi in batter or fish fingers, grilled, chopped and spiked on to kebab skewers

Gabrielle De Pauw · Slough

Curried Cheese Balls

100g (4oz) English Cheddar cheese, grated
50g (2oz) English butter, softened
50g (2oz) fresh white breadcrumbs
1 level teaspoon curry powder
50g (2oz) desiccated coconut
cocktail sticks

1 Mix together the cheese, butter, breadcrumbs and curry powder. Beat until thoroughly combined

2 Divide into small balls about the size of a hazelnut and coat with the desiccated coconut

3 Chill slightly, then serve on cocktail sticks

4 These cheese balls can be arranged very attractively on a bed of shredded lettuce or in a bright napkin in a basket

Makes about 20

Mrs J. James · Gloucester

Cheese Oatcakes

225g (8oz) medium oatmeal
75g (3oz) English Cheddar cheese, grated
¼ level teaspoon salt
¼ level teaspoon baking powder
2 teaspoons melted bacon fat or English butter
6 tablespoons warm water

1 Mix the oatmeal, cheese, salt and baking powder together. Stir in the bacon fat or butter and the warm water to make a soft dough. Knead lightly

2 Roll out on a lightly floured work top to 0·5cm (¼ inch) thick and cut into small squares, 5cm (2 inch) rounds using a biscuit cutter, or triangle shape

3 Heat a heavy-based frying pan or griddle and grease very lightly with butter. Cook the oatcakes until browned on one side, then turn over and cook until browned on the second side. Cool on a wire rack

4 Alternatively the oatcakes can be baked. Place them on buttered baking sheets and bake in the oven at 200°C (400°F), mark 6, for 20–25 minutes. Cool on a wire rack

5 Serve cold, buttered. Garlic or chive butter tastes very good with these oatcakes

Makes about 12

M. C. Nicol · Morden

To prepare cheese and biscuits quickly

Grate the cheese on to a plate. Butter the biscuits and dip each one into the cheese

Mrs P. A. Gregory · Orpington

Cheese and Fish Pâté

100g (4oz) mature English Cheddar cheese, finely grated
100g (4oz) English butter, softened
2 tablespoons natural yogurt
200-g (7½-oz) can cods roes, drained
1 teaspoon Tabasco sauce
1 level teaspoon made English mustard
1 level teaspoon celery salt
1 level teaspoon garlic powder
1 tablespoon finely chopped fresh parsley
1 level teaspoon paprika
1 tablespoon mayonnaise
1 tablespoon lemon juice
few peeled shrimps or prawns (optional)
lemon slices, havled

1 Beat the cheese, butter and yogurt together until thoroughly combined, then beat in the cods roes and remaining ingredients, except shrimps and lemon slices

2 Spoon the pâté into 1 large serving dish or 6 individual ramekins or small bowls and chill lightly

3 Garnish with a few peeled shrimps or prawns (if liked) and halved lemon slices. Serve immediately with hot toast fingers

Serves 6

Mrs F. M. Thatche · Wells

English Apple Fondue

1 small garlic clove, skinned and halved
450ml (¾ pint) apple juice
1 level tablespoon cornflour
¼ level teaspoon dry mustard
¼ level teaspoon paprika
700g (1½lb) English Cheddar cheese, grated
4–6 dessert apples, peeled, cored and cubed
a selection of celery, cauliflower florets
French bread to serve

1 Rub the inside of a heavy fondue pan with the cut side of each half of the garlic clove

2 Mix a little apple juice into the cornflour, mustard and paprika to form a smooth consistency

3 Warm the remaining juice in the fondue pan, gradually add the cheese, stirring continuously over low heat until melted. Stir in the cornflour mixture and bring gently to the boil, and continue stirring off the heat for a further minute until smooth. Do not overcook otherwise the mixture will separate

4 Transfer the pan to a spirit lamp or fondue burner, on a large table mat on the dining table

5 Serve cubes of dessert apples, tossed in lemon juice, or pieces of celery, cauliflower florets, or cubes of French bread, to dip in the hot cheese sauce. Warn your guests that the cheese fondue is very hot

Serves 4–6

Mrs M. Ashworth · Enfield

Left to right: Cheese Oatcakes, Cheese and Fish Pâté, English Apple Fondue

Cheese Starlets

175g (6oz) English butter
150g (5oz) English Cheddar cheese, grated
175g (6oz) plain flour
1 level teaspoon paprika
1 level teaspoon salt
4 level tablespoons sesame seeds

1 Cream together the butter and cheese until soft, pale and very creamy

2 Sift the flour, paprika and salt together, then gradually beat these ingredients into the creamed mixture with half the sesame seeds

3 Fit a large star nozzle into a piping bag. Using two-thirds of the mixture pipe small star biscuits on to ungreased baking sheets

4 Roll the reserved dough into tiny balls, then coat in the remaining sesame seeds. Top each of the piped biscuits with one of these balls, pressing it in to form a flower shape

5 Bake in the oven at 180°C (350°F), mark 4, for 12–15 minutes, or until very lightly browned. Cool on a wire rack

Makes 60–70

These biscuits freeze well: pack them in rigid containers and remove them from the freezer about 1–2 hours before you wish to serve them

Linda Johnson · Farnborough Cove

Cheddar Puffs

50g (2oz) English butter
150ml (¼ pint) water
65g (2½oz) plain flour, sifted
2 eggs, lightly beaten
6 tablespoons medium sherry
175g (6oz) English Cheddar cheese, finely grated

1 Put the butter and water together in a saucepan and heat gently until the butter melts, then bring quickly to the boil. Pour in the flour all at once, remove from heat and beat hard for a few seconds until the mixture forms a smooth paste which leaves the sides of the pan clean. Leave to cool for about 5 minutes

2 Gradually beat in the eggs and continue to beat hard for 1–2 minutes until smooth and very glossy

3 Place teaspoonfuls of the mixture on to buttered baking sheets and bake in the oven at 200°C (400°F), mark 6, for about 15 minutes, until well puffed and golden brown

4 Meanwhile prepare the filling by beating the sherry and cheese together to make a smooth paste

5 Immediately the puffs are cooked, cut a slit in them to allow the steam to escape and leave to cool on a wire rack

6 Spoon or pipe the filling into the puffs and serve within a couple of hours of filling or the pastry will become soft

Makes about 30

L. N. Thorogood · Wokingham

Top to bottom: Cheese Starlets, Cheddar Puffs, Stilton Medallions

Stilton Medallions

1 egg yolk
125g (5oz) English butter, softened
100g (4oz) plain flour, sifted
50g (2oz) White Stilton cheese, crumbled
salt and freshly ground pepper
dry mustard
100g (4oz) Blue Stilton cheese, finely grated or crumbled

1 To make the biscuits, beat the egg yolk into 75g (3oz) butter, then stir in the flour, White Stilton, seasoning and mustard to taste

2 Knead the mixture to form a smooth dough, then roll out thinly on a lightly floured work top

3 Cut out 2·5cm (1 inch) circles with a plain biscuit cutter. Place slightly apart on a baking sheet and bake in the oven at 200°C (400°F), mark 6, for about 10 minutes until golden brown. Cool on a wire rack

4 Meanwhile, prepare the filling. Beat the remaining butter and Blue Stilton together until soft and thoroughly combined

5 Taste the filling and add seasoning to taste. Spoon the creamed cheese and butter mixture into a piping bag fitted with a star nozzle

6 Pipe a rosette of cheese mixture on each of the biscuits, then press together in pairs with a rosette on top. Alternatively, the filling may be spread on the biscuits with a knife

Makes 24 pairs

Mrs P. Hall · Keighley

Cheese and Mint Saddies

215-g (7½-oz) packet frozen puff pastry, thawed
100g (4oz) Lancashire cheese, grated or crumbled
1 hard-boiled egg, chopped
2 teaspoons finely chopped fresh mint
2—3 tablespoons fresh single cream
salt and freshly ground pepper
pinch of dry mustard
beaten egg

1 Roll out the pastry to 0·5cm (¼ inch) thick on a lightly floured work top. Use a 10cm (4 inch) plain cutter to cut out 16—18 pastry circles

2 Mix the cheese, egg, mint and fresh cream together. Season to taste and add a pinch of mustard. Divide this mixture equally between the pastry circles

3 Brush the edges of the pastry with a little beaten egg and fold them up to meet in the middle, over the filling. Press firmly together to seal

4 Turn the saddies sideways and flatten with a rolling pin

5 Place on wetted baking sheets. Make two cuts in the top of each and brush with beaten egg

6 Bake in the oven at 220°C (425°F), mark 7, for 20—25 minutes until puffed and golden brown

Makes 16—18

Mrs E. Johnson · Blackpool

Leicester Apple Pasties

215-g (7½-oz) packet frozen puff pastry, thawed
2 dessert apples, peeled and cored
juice of 1 lemon
150g (5oz) Leicester cheese, cubed
25g (1oz) raisins, soaked in 3 tablespoons sherry or dry white wine
beaten egg
caster sugar

1 Roll out the pastry on a lightly floured work top. Use a 7·5cm (3 inch) biscuit cutter to cut out pastry circles

2 Finely dice the apples and toss them in the lemon juice to keep white

3 Mix the cheese and apples with the raisins and sherry or wine and divide this mixture between the pastry circles

4 Brush the edges of the pastry with beaten egg and fold them together over the filling in a pastry shape. Press the edges together firmly to seal in the filling and pinch the pastry to make an attractive and neat border

5 Brush with beaten egg and place slightly apart on a greased baking sheet. Bake in the oven at 190°C (375°F), mark 5, for 20 minutes, or until well puffed and golden brown

6 Serve on paper doilies, dredged with a little caster sugar

Rose-Marie Varndell · Portsmouth

Stilton Pyramids

4 eggs, hard boiled
100g (4oz) Blue Stilton cheese
75g (3oz) English butter
8 open mushrooms
2 tablespoons French dressing
parsley sprigs
4 gherkins, sliced
2 tomatoes, sliced

1 Remove the yolks from the hard-boiled eggs and blend with the cheese and butter to a smooth paste

2 Remove the stalks from the mushrooms and toss the mushroom heads in the French dressing. Arrange, dark-side uppermost, on a plate

3 Place the cheese mixture in a piping bag and make a pyramid in the centre of each mushroom. Top with a small sprig of parsley

4 Chop the egg whites and arrange on the serving plate with the gherkins and tomatoes

Serves 4

Mrs M. A. Williams · Plymouth

Wensleydale Soufflé Tarts

225g (8oz) shortcrust pastry made with 225g (8oz) plain flour (page 116)
100g (4oz) cooked ham, minced
1 level teaspoon mild French mustard
15g (½oz) English butter
20g (¾oz) plain flour
100ml (4 fl oz) milk
50g (2oz) Wensleydale cheese, grated
2 eggs, separated
salt and freshly ground white pepper
a little freshly grated nutmeg

1 Make up shortcrust pastry (page 116)

2 Roll out on a lightly floured work top and line six 7·5cm (3 inch) loose-bottomed tart tins.

3 Bake 'blind' for 10 minutes in the oven at 200°C (400°F), mark 6, then reduce the temperature to 180°C (350°F), mark 4, and bake for a further 10 minutes

4 Mix the cooked ham with the mustard and spread evenly between the pastry bases

5 Place butter, flour and milk in a saucepan; heat stirring continuously until the sauce thickens, boils and is smooth

6 Remove the pan from the heat and gradually beat in the cheese and egg yolks. Add seasoning and nutmeg to taste. Cover the surface of the sauce with a piece of buttered greaseproof paper to prevent a skin forming, and leave to cool

7 Whisk the egg whites until they stand in soft peaks. Stir about one-third into the sauce, then carefully fold the remainder in, taking care not to expel all the air

8 Pour the soufflé into the pastry tarts and bake in the oven at 220°C (425°F), mark 7, for 15 minutes or until well risen and golden brown

Serves 6

Mrs E. Chetwynd · Hatfield

Cheese and Onion Pinwheels

215-g (7½-oz) packet frozen puff pastry, thawed
2 level teaspoons dried oregano
225g (8oz) mature English Cheddar cheese, grated
1 medium onion, skinned and grated
salt and freshly ground pepper

1 Roll out the pastry thinly into an oblong shape – about 25·5 × 30·5cm (10 × 12 inches)

2 Sprinkle the oregano over the pastry. Mix the cheese with the onion, season to taste and spread evenly over the pastry. Roll up tightly from the longer side and cut into 1cm (½ inch) thick slices

3 Lay the pinwheels on dampened baking sheets and bake in the oven at 180°C (350°F), mark 4, for about 20 minutes until puffed and golden. Serve hot or cold

Makes about 24

Mrs B. Jones · Wallasey

Cheshire Walnut Tartlets

100g (4oz) English Cheshire, grated
1 egg yolk
salt and freshly ground pepper
dry mustard
15g (½oz) English butter, softened
50g (2oz) walnuts, chopped
215-g (7½-oz) packet frozen puff pastry, thawed
2 egg whites

1 Mix the cheese with the egg yolk. Add the seasoning and mustard to taste, then beat in the butter and walnuts

2 Roll out the pastry thinly and use to line 20–24 patty tins. Prick the pastry all over with a fork

3 Whisk the egg whites until they stand in stiff peaks. Stir a little into the cheese mixture, then fold in the remainder

4 Place a little of the cheese mixture in each pastry case and bake in the oven at 200°C (400°F), mark 6, for about 20 minutes, until well risen and golden brown. Serve hot

Makes 20–24

Margaret Mulvana · Doncaster

Cheese Basket Tarts

175g (6oz) shortcrust pastry made with 175g (6oz) plain flour (page 116)
15g (½oz) plain flour
15g (½oz) English butter
150ml (¼ pint) milk
1 egg, separated
50g (2oz) English Cheddar cheese, grated
salt
cayenne

1 Make up the shortcrust pastry (page 116)

2 Roll out the pastry thinly on a lightly floured work top. Reserve about one-eighth of pastry for the trimmings; use remaining pastry to line 18 patty tins

3 Place the flour, butter and milk in a saucepan; then heat, stirring continuously, until the sauce thickens, boils and is smooth. Cook for 1 minute

4 Remove the pan from the heat and add the egg yolk, grated cheese, salt to taste and a little cayenne. Stir until the cheese melts

5 Whisk the egg white until it stands in stiff peaks, then fold into the sauce. Put a heaped teaspoon of this mixture into each of the pastry cases. Cut thin strips of the reserved pastry and place a strip across each tart

6 Bake in the oven at 200°C (400°F), mark 6, for 15–20 minutes, until well risen and golden. The cooked tarts will resemble miniature soufflés in a basket. Serve hot

Makes 18

Mrs J. Wilbor · Northallerton

Stilton Croquettes

50g (2oz) celery, chopped
100g (4oz) English butter
100g (4oz) plain flour
300ml (½ pint) milk
salt and pepper
2 egg yolks
50g (2oz) tomatoes, skinned, seeded and finely chopped
100g (4oz) Blue Stilton cheese, mashed
flour
1 egg, beaten
toasted breadcrumbs
oil, to fry
watercress sprigs

1 Sauté the celery in butter until soft

2 Stir in the flour and cook for 1 to 2 minutes, stirring all the time. Gradually add the milk, bring to the boil and season to taste

3 Stir in the egg yolks, tomatoes, cheese and mix well. Spread on to a tray or plate and chill for 30 minutes

4 Shape the mixture into balls and coat with flour. Brush with egg and toss in breadcrumbs. Deep fry until golden, drain well and serve garnished with watercress

Serves 4

Susan Andrews · Birstall

Top: Cheese and Onion Pinwheels. Bottom left: Cheshire Walnut Tartlets. Bottom right: Stilton Croquettes

Savoury Palmiers

215-g (7½-oz) packet frozen puff pastry, thawed
75g (3oz) English Cheddar cheese, grated
milk
paprika

1 Roll out pastry to form a rectangle measuring 25·5 × 30·5cm (10 × 12 inches). Sprinkle about a quarter of the grated cheese evenly over the surface. Fold the long sides in to meet in the middle and enclose the cheese

2 Sprinkle a second quarter of the cheese over the top of the folded pastry. Again fold the long sides of the pastry in to meet in the middle

3 Sprinkle half the remaining cheese on top and fold in half. Press together with a rolling pin

4 Cut into thin slices and place, cut side up, on a baking sheet. Allow space between the slices for spreading. Brush with a little milk, sprinkle the remaining cheese over and bake in the oven at 220°C (425°F), mark 7, for 15 to 20 minutes. Serve dusted with paprika

Makes 20—24

Mrs M. Hughes · Coventry

Left to right: Cheddicks, Cheese and Almond Sablés, Walnut Cheese Savouries, Savoury Palmiers

Cashew Savouries

100g (4oz) self-raising flour
100g (4oz) English butter, softened
75g (3oz) English Cheddar cheese, grated
salt and freshly ground pepper
pinch of paprika
pinch of nutmeg
25g (1oz) roasted cashew nuts, chopped
beaten egg
bunch of watercress, trimmed and washed
sticks of celery

1 Mix the flour with the butter, cheese, seasoning, paprika, nutmeg and cashew nuts. Knead all the ingredients together to form a dough

2 Divide the dough into 20 equal portions — this is easier if the dough is first formed into a large roll, then cut into equal slices

3 Form each portion into a small roll about 1cm (½ inch) thick. Place on lightly buttered baking sheets and flatten each with a fork

4 Brush with beaten egg and bake in the oven at 180°C (350°F), mark 4, for 15—20 minutes

5 Serve hot or cool on a wire rack and serve cold. A bowl of watercress and pieces of celery are the ideal accompaniments for these savouries

Makes 20

Miss E. R. Friend · Otley

Walnut Cheese Savouries

50g (4oz) plain flour
75g (3oz) English butter
75g (3oz) English Cheddar cheese, grated
salt and freshly ground pepper
1 egg, beaten
25g (1oz) walnuts, coarsely chopped
½ level teaspoon sea or coarse salt

1 Sift the flour into a bowl and rub in the butter, cut in pieces, until the mixture resembles fine breadcrumbs

2 Add the cheese and seasoning to taste. Knead well to form the ingredients into a dough. Roll out on a well-floured work top to 0·25cm (⅛ inch) into 5cm (2 inch) wide strips. Trim the edges if necessary

3 Place the biscuits on baking sheets lined with greaseproof paper. Brush with the beaten egg. Top with chopped walnuts and coarse salt

4 Cut each strip into small triangle shapes and ease them apart. Bake in the oven at 200°C (400°F), mark 6, for about 10 minutes, or until golden brown

5 Cool on a wire rack and store in an airtight tin

Makes about 36

Mrs G. H. Bradburn · Sutton Coldfield

Cheese and Almond Sablés

175g (6oz) plain flour
275g (10oz) English butter
40g (1½oz) ground almonds
175g (6oz) English Cheddar cheese, grated
2 egg yolks
pinch of salt
½ level teaspoon paprika
1–2 tablespoons cold water
beaten egg
40g (1½oz) toasted almonds, finely chopped

1 Sift the flour into a bowl, add 100g (4oz) butter, cut into pieces and rub until the mixture resembles fine breadcrumbs

2 Add the ground almonds and grated cheese. Make a well in the centre of the dry ingredients, add the egg yolks, salt and paprika with enough cold water to mix to a soft pastry dough

3 Knead until a smooth paste and chill before using. Roll out to 0·25cm (⅛ inch) thick on a lightly floured work top. Using 4cm (1½ inch) plain cutter, cut out rounds

4 Place the biscuits slightly apart on greased baking sheets. Brush with beaten egg and bake in the oven at 200°C (400°F), mark 6, for about 10 minutes or until golden. Cool on a wire rack

5 Blend remaining butter with toasted chopped almonds and sandwich biscuits in pairs with the almond butter

Makes about 72 small biscuits

D. J. Sutherland · Braintree

Cheddicks

1 medium slice of white bread, with crusts removed
25g (1oz) English butter
25g (1oz) self-raising flour
50g (2oz) mature English Cheddar cheese, grated
salt and freshly ground pepper
about 2 tablespoons cold water

1 Place the slice of bread in the oven at 200°C (400°F), mark 6, for about 10–25 minutes, until dark golden but not burnt. Cool, then crush, in a polythene bag, with a rolling pin

2 Rub the butter into the flour until the mixture resembles fine breadcrumbs. Add all the other ingredients and stir in sufficient cold water to bind into a short pastry dough

3 Roll out the dough on a floured work top to about 0·5cm (⅛ inch) thick. Cut into about 36 sticks

4 Place the sticks on a buttered sheet and bake in the oven at 200°C (400°F), mark 6, for about 10 minutes, until lightly browned

5 Cool on a wire rack

Makes about 36

Mrs M. Ward · Ascot

Children's Favourites

For those with healthy appetites, dishes with cheese will satisfy the children's hunger pangs. But for those less enthusiastic about food, they will need to be coaxed with some new and exciting ideas. The dishes in this chapter have been voted winners by the youngsters who tried them and in the view of the mum who made them 'it was marvellous to have such ingenious ideas to make up, and a treat to see the children's faces when they were served. At least I was sure that they were enjoying a really nutritious dish.'

Yellow Submarine

1 long bread roll
pickle or relish
1 banana
1 rasher of bacon, rinded and grilled
1 sausage, grilled and cut in half lengthways
40g (1½oz) English Cheddar cheese, grated
extra cube of cheese
tomato slice

1 Split the bread roll open along the top but do not cut right through. Spread with pickle or relish

2 Cut the banana in half lengthways and lay one half along the inside of each cut edge of the opened roll

3 Sandwich the bacon and sausage between the cut banana and partly close the roll together

4 Sprinkle the cheese on top and place under a hot grill until bubbling and golden

5 Secure a periscope-shaped piece of cheese with a cocktail stick on top of the submarine and a propeller-shaped piece of tomato on the end

Makes 1 Yellow Submarine

Nicola J. Reeve · Bristol

Bangers in Bunk Beds

225g (8oz) plain flour
salt and freshly ground pepper
100g (4oz) English butter
175g (6oz) English Cheddar cheese, grated
1 level teaspoon dried parsley
2 eggs
pinch of dry mustard
8 chipolata sausages
68-g (2½-oz) packet instant potato
knob of butter
1 tablespoon tomato ketchup
16 cocktail sticks
227-g (8-oz) can baked beans (optional)
227-g (8-oz) can garden peas, drained

1 Sift the flour, salt and pepper to taste into a bowl, add the butter, cut into pieces, and rub it into the dry ingredients until the mixture resembles fine breadcrumbs

2 Stir 100g (4oz) of the cheese into the mixture, then add the parsley. Beat the eggs with the mustard and pour into the dry mixture, stirring to form a dough.

Left to right: Yellow Submarine, Bangers in Bunk Beds, Cheesy Charlie Clown

3 Roll out on a floured work top and cut into 8 rectangles a little wider and longer than the chipolata sausages. These rectangles will represent the beds

4 Place the pastry rectangles on baking sheets, prick them all over with a fork and bake in the oven at 200°C (400°F), mark 6, for 15–20 minutes

5 Grill the chipolata sausages. Make up the instant potato as directed on packet. Add the knob of butter, tomato ketchup and remaining cheese. Stir until smooth and evenly coloured

6 Put a spoonful of potato at one end of the pastry beds to represent pillows. Rest a chipolata sausage on each and cover, as far up as the head on the pillow, with a thin layer of potato. Mark the blanket texture on the potato with a fork

7 Stick cocktail sticks through each corner of the lower bunks and press the upper bunks on top so that the points just show through. Stick a pea or bean on the top of each cocktail stick to represent a bed-post. Return the beds to the oven for 5 minutes to heat through

8 Heat the baked beans and the peas. Arrange the peas or beans and peas in a pattern on 4 large plates to represent bedside rugs and place the bunk beds beside them. Serve immediately

Serves 4

This is a very novel idea for the mum with the time, particularly if the children are 'off their food'

L. A. Every · Weymouth

Cheesy Charlie Clown

1 thick slice of white or wheatmeal bread
15g (½oz) English butter
2 slices of hard-boiled egg
2 raisins
1 slice of cucumber
1 radish
1 thick slice of Double Gloucester cheese
2 thick slices of English Cheddar cheese
mustard and cress, washed

1 Remove crusts and trim the slice of bread into a shape to resemble a face. Butter the bread and place on a large, flat plate

2 Arrange the egg slices on the bread to represent eyes and raisins for pupils. Cut the slice of cucumber in half and trim each piece into a crescent shape. Place one of these cucumber crescents above each eye in the form of a quizzical eyebrow

3 Charlie's red nose is simply the radish half, placed neatly in position. To make the big smiley mouth, cut the shape from the Double Gloucester cheese

4 Cut large bow tie from one of the slices of Cheddar cheese; cut out a triangular hat from the second slice

5 Trim the cress stems short before arranging them around the top of the clown's head. Put on his cheese hat and add the bow tie with spots made from remaining radish

Makes 1 Charlie Clown

Mrs M. E. Whittaker · Blackpool

Cheese with Crisps

40g (1½oz) plain flour
25g (1oz) English butter
600ml (1 pint) milk
salt and freshly ground black pepper
150g (5oz) English Cheddar cheese, grated
2 hard-boiled eggs, sliced
227-g (8-oz) can mixed vegetables, drained
100g (4oz) cooked cold meat, diced
1 small red pepper, seeded and finely chopped
2 small packets potato crisps, crushed
a few red pepper rings (optional)
tomato slices (optional)

1 Place the flour, butter and milk in a saucepan; heat, stirring continuously until the sauce thickens, boils and is smooth. Cook for 1 minute. Season sparingly with salt and pepper

2 Remove the pan from the heat, add 100g (4oz) of the cheese and stir, off the heat, until it has melted

3 Pour a little of the sauce into an ovenproof casserole and arrange the eggs on top. Add the vegetables, meat and red pepper to the remaining sauce

4 Pour the sauce over the eggs. Mix the crushed crisps with the remaining cheese and sprinkle on top. Bake in the oven at 180°C (350°F), mark 4, for about 30 minutes, until golden brown

5 Garnish with rings of red pepper or tomato slices. Serve immediately

Serves 2–4

E. Parsons · Burford

Cheese and Peanut Croquettes

150g (5oz) fresh white breadcrumbs
1 medium onion, skinned and grated
100g (4oz) mature English Cheddar cheese, grated
1 level teaspoon dried parsley or 2 teaspoons chopped
  fresh parsley
¾ level teaspoon dry mustard
salt and freshly ground pepper
1 egg yolk
1 egg white, lightly whisked
75g (3oz) salted peanuts, finely chopped
vegetable oil for shallow frying
bunch of watercress, washed and trimmed

1 Place the breadcrumbs in a large mixing bowl with the grated onion, cheese and parsley

2 Add the dry mustard, salt and pepper to taste, then stir in the egg yolk to bind the ingredients together

3 Divide the mixture into 12–14 equal portions and roll each into a sausage shape. Dip these croquettes first

into the egg white, then coat them evenly with the peanuts. Place on a plate, cover and leave in the refrigerator until well chilled

4 Heat about 2 tablespoons of oil in a frying pan and gently fry the croquettes, turning occasionally until crisp and golden. Take care that the oil does not become to hot or the peanut coating may overcook

5 Drain on crumpled absorbent kitchen paper. Arrange the croquettes on a serving plate and garnish with watercress. Serve immediately with baked potatoes or a tomato salad

Serves 4

Miss D. Britton · Bristol

Crunchy Chicken 'n' Cheese

175g (6oz) cold cooked chicken, diced
50g (2oz) English butter
2 medium onions, skinned and chopped
3 sticks of celery, chopped
50g (2oz) salted peanuts
2 level teaspoons plain flour
300ml (½ pint) milk
100g (4oz) English Cheddar cheese, grated
small packet crisps, salted or flavoured if preferred
1 tablespoon chopped fresh parsley

1 Place the chicken in a small pie dish

2 Melt the butter in a saucepan and fry the onions in it until soft but not browned

3 Add celery and peanuts and continue to cook for 2–3 minutes. Stir in the flour and cook for a further 1–2 minutes

4 Gradually stir the milk into the mixture and cook gently, stirring continuously, until the sauce thickens

5 Stir half the cheese into the sauce and pour over chicken. Mix the remaining cheese with the crisps and sprinkle over the top

6 Bake in the oven at 200°C (400°F), mark 6, for 30 minutes until crisp and golden

7 Sprinkle with chopped parsley and serve immediately

Serves 3–4

Mrs E. E. Simpson · Eastbourne

To 'take away the horrid taste' of medicine, pop a cube of English cheese in the mouth. Better than a sweet for the teeth and the waistline

Mrs J. M. Stenning · Goring-by-Sea

Devilled Pizza

225g (8oz) wholemeal flour
pinch of salt
2 level teaspoons baking powder
50g (2oz) English butter
150ml (¼ pint) milk
350g (12oz) luncheon meat, chopped
175g (6oz) English Cheddar cheese, finely grated
1 small onion, skinned and finely chopped
1 small green pepper, seeded and finely chopped
3 tablespoons tomato ketchup
1 tablespoon made mustard
salt and freshly ground pepper
green pepper slices

1 To make the base, mix the flour, salt and baking powder together in a large bowl. Add the butter, cut into pieces, and rub it into the dry ingredients until the mixture resembles fine breadcrumbs

2 Add the milk and mix to form a soft dough. Knead very lightly until smooth

3 Roll out the dough on a lightly floured work top, and use to line the base of a 30·5 × 20·5cm (12 × 8 inch) buttered Swiss roll tin

4 To prepare the filling, mix all the remaining ingredients except the green pepper, adding seasoning to taste

5 Spread the filling evenly over the scone base and bake in the oven at 200°C (400°F), mark 6, for 25 minutes, until golden brown. Serve hot or cold garnished with sliced pepper

Serves 4

Mrs B. Whitaker · Sheffield

Cheesy Oatburgers

175g (6oz) Leicester cheese, grated
1 small green pepper, seeded and finely chopped
1 large tomato, skinned and finely chopped
1 small onion, skinned and finely chopped
100g (4oz) porridge oats
2 eggs
salt and freshly ground pepper
2–4 tablespoons vegetable oil for shallow frying

1 Reserve 50g (2oz) of the cheese for topping. Mix the remaining cheese with the pepper, tomato, onion and oats. Add the eggs and mix thoroughly until well blended. Season generously to taste

2 Divide the mixture into 4 or 6 portions and shape each into a burger. If the mixture is a little sticky add more oats so that it binds together well

3 Heat about 2 tablespoons of oil in a frying pan and gently fry the burgers until golden brown. Turn them carefully with a large spatula and continue cooking until golden on the second side. Add a little more oil if necessary

4 Sprinkle the reserved cheese over the burgers and place under a hot grill until the top is golden brown

5 Serve immediately with the children's favourite accompaniments

Makes 4 large or 6 small burgers

Miss Linda Hyde · Bridford

Left: Devilled Pizza. Right: Cheesy Oatburgers

Fish Lasagne

6 sheets lasagne
65g (2 ½ oz) plain flour
65g (2 ½ oz) English butter
750ml (1 ¼ pints) milk
150g (5oz) English Cheddar cheese, grated
2 tablespoons chopped fresh parsley
salt and freshly ground pepper
225–250g (8–10oz) white fish fillets, cooked, skinned and flaked
tomato slices (optional)
sprigs of parsley (optional)

1 Cook the lasagne according to the instructions on the packet

2 To make a cheese sauce, place the flour, butter and milk in a saucepan; heat, stirring continuously, until the sauce thickens, boils and is smooth. Cook for 1 minute. Remove the pan from the heat, add all but 25g (1oz) of the cheese and stir, off the heat, until it has melted

3 Add the chopped parsley and season to taste

4 Arrange layers of the cooked lasagne, cheese sauce and fish in a buttered, oblong ovenproof dish. Start with a layer of lasagne and finish with a layer of cheese sauce. Remove any small bones from the fish as you add it to the dish

5 Sprinkle the reserved cheese on top and bake in the oven at 190°C (375°F), mark 5, for about 30 minutes, until golden brown and bubbling hot

6 The lasagne may be garnished with tomato slices and sprigs of parsley, then served immediately

Serves 4–6

J. Keen · Stirling

Left to right: Fish Lasagne, Cheesy Fishing Smacks, Fish Finger Bake, Golden Fingers

Cheesy Fishing Smacks

4 large potatoes
50g (2oz) English butter
100g (4oz) English Cheddar cheese, finely grated
225g (8oz) smoked haddock fillet cooked, skinned and flaked
salt and freshly ground pepper
a little milk
4 slices of Double Gloucester cheese, cut into 8 triangles
8 cocktail sticks
tomato slices (optional)

1 Bake the potatoes in the oven at 190°C (375°F), mark 5, until soft – about 1 ½ –2 hours

2 Split the cooked potatoes in half then scoop out the potato and mash with the butter, cheese, fish and seasoning to taste. Add a little milk to soften the mixture if necessary

3 Spoon the fish mixture back into potato shells and return them to the oven for 10 minutes

4 Fix each triangle of cheese on a cocktail stick and stand in each potato to represent a sail

5 For colour, these boats can be garnish with halved tomato slices if liked

Serves 4

Other toppings to serve on jacket potatoes are: grated English Cheddar cheese and sautéed mushrooms; crumbled Lancashire cheese with crisp, fried bacon; Double Gloucester cheese with a spoonful of pickle; grated Leicester cheese with a sprinkling of chopped chives

Mrs M. I. Bowyer · Birmingham

Fish Finger Bake

10 fish fingers, thawed
lemon juice
salt and finely ground pepper
50g (2oz) English butter
1 large onion, skinned and finely chopped
1 red or green pepper, seeded and chopped (optional)
50g (2oz) button mushrooms, sliced
425-g (15-oz) can tomatoes
100g (4oz) English Cheddar cheese, grated
lemon twist
parsley sprigs

1 Butter 20·5–23cm (8–9 inch) ovenproof dish and arrange the fish fingers in the bottom. Sprinkle generously with lemon juice and season with salt and pepper to taste

2 Melt half the butter in a saucepan, add the onion and pepper (if used) and cook for a few minutes. Stir in the mushrooms and continue to cook until the onion becomes soft but not browned

3 Add the tomatoes and remove the pan from the heat. Stir well

4 Pour this mixture over the fish fingers and finally top with the grated cheese

5 Dot with the remaining butter, cut into small pieces, and bake in the oven at 220°C (425°F), mark 7, about 35 minutes until cooked and golden brown

6 Serve garnished with lemon twist and parsley sprigs

Serves 4–5

Mrs Patricia Gregory · Orpington

Golden Fingers

215-g (7½-oz) packet frozen puff pastry, thawed
2 tablespoons tomato ketchup
10 frozen fish fingers, thawed but chilled
100g (4oz) Leicester cheese
a little beaten egg

1 Roll out the pastry to a rectangle measuring 38 × 25·5cm (15 × 10 inches)

2 Spread the ketchup over the pastry, leaving a 1cm (½ inch) border all around the edge. Lay the fish fingers about 1cm (½ inch) apart to one side down the longer edge

3 Cut the cheese into 10 equal pieces and place 1 piece on top of each fish finger. Carefully fold the pastry edge opposite the fish fingers over the top, to enclose the fingers completely. Seal the edges by pressing the pastry firmly together

4 Cut down through the pastry between the fish fingers and place them, slightly apart, on a dampened baking sheet

5 Brush with a little beaten egg and bake in the oven at 230°C (450°F), mark 8, for about 20 minutes, until the pastry is well puffed and golden brown

6 Serve hot with chips and peas, or cold for school lunches and picnics

Makes 10

Mrs P. A. Saunders · Bournemouth

Crispy Cheddar Chips

450g (1lb) potatoes, peeled
25g (1oz) English butter
100g (4oz) English Cheddar cheese, grated
salt and freshly ground black pepper

1 Cut the potatoes into neat chips

2 Melt the butter in a saucepan. Add the cheese and plenty of salt and pepper, then add the chips. Put the lid on the pan and shake it gently so that the chips are well coated with both the butter and cheese

3 Turn the chips into a shallow ovenproof dish and bake in the oven at 190°C (375°F), mark 5, for 50–60 minutes, until tender and crisp on the outside

4 Serve immediately with fish fingers and baked beans

Serves 3–4

Miss Nadine Andrew · Sydenham

Mixed Vegetable and Cheese Rice

1 tablespoon vegetable oil
1 tablespoon finely chopped onion
1 medium carrot, peeled and finely chopped
2 sticks celery, finely chopped
227-g (8-oz) can tomatoes
150ml (¼ pint) water
1 tablespoon brown rice
pinch of salt
50g (2oz) English Cheddar or Caerphilly cheese, grated

1 Heat the oil in a small saucepan, then add the onion and cook until soft but not browned

2 Add the carrot and celery, stir and cook gently for 2–3 minutes. Pour in the tomatoes and their juice together with the water

3 Bring to the boil, then add the rice and a pinch of salt. Cover and simmer until the vegetables and rice are cooked – about 35 minutes

4 When cooked, add the cheese and either liquidise or mash according to the requirements of your children

Makes 3 portions

This dish is suitable for serving to young children over the age of 9 months

Mrs Wendy Loxley · Cranleigh

Tasty Cheshire Buns

225g (8oz) self-raising flour
pinch of salt
75g (3oz) English butter
75g (3oz) English Cheshire cheese, grated
75g (3oz) sultanas
2 eggs, beaten
1 teaspoon yeast extract
5–7 tablespoons milk

1 Sift the flour and salt into a bowl. Add the butter, cut in pieces, and rub it into the flour until the mixture resembles fine breadcrumbs

2 Add the cheese and sultanas to the mixture, then mix in the eggs, yeast extract and sufficient milk to make a stiff dough

3 Quickly and very lightly, knead the dough together, then divide it in half. Cut each half into 10 equal portions and place them in paper bun cases on a baking sheet

4 Bake the buns in the oven at 190°C (375°F), mark 5, for 15–20 minutes, until risen and golden brown

5 Cool on a wire rack. Serve with a glass of milk for a light lunch or nourishing snack

Makes 20 buns

Mrs S. A. Mobbs · Plymouth

Hot Cheese Rolls

90-g (3½-oz) can tuna, drained
175g (6oz) English Cheddar cheese, grated
½ small onion, skinned and finely chopped
½ green pepper, seeded and finely chopped
75g (3oz) English butter, melted
2 tablespoons tomato ketchup
8 crusty bread rolls

1 Flake the tuna with a fork and mix it with the cheese, onion and pepper. Add 50g (2oz) butter and the tomato ketchup

2 Cut off and reserve the tops of the rolls. Scoop out the soft centre – this can be dried, reduced to crumbs and stored in an airtight jar for future use

3 Spoon the cheese mixture into the crusty shells, to within 1cm (½ inch) of the rim. Brush the remaining butter over the cut side of the tops and replace them on the rolls

4 Wrap the cheese rolls in foil and bake in the oven at 190°C (375°F), mark 5, for about 20 minutes until the cheese filling has melted and is bubbling hot. Serve immediately

Serves 8

Joyce I. Griffin · Maidenhead

Left to right: Tasty Cheshire Buns, Cheddar Chompies, The 'Guess-What's-In-It' Fudge

Cheddar Chompies

50g (2oz) English butter, softened
50g (2oz) soft brown sugar
1 egg
100g (4oz) plain flour
50g (2oz) bran flakes
50g (2oz) desiccated coconut
350g (12oz) English Cheddar cheese, grated
generous pinch of dry mustard
salt and freshly ground pepper
pinch of cayenne

1 Place all the ingredients in a large bowl and mix together with a wooden spoon to form a dough

2 Knead the dough thoroughly until smooth and pliable, then roll out thinly on a floured work top

3 Cut out the biscuits into 6·5cm (2½ inch) squares, place them slightly apart on lightly greased baking sheets and bake in the oven at 180°C (350°F), mark 4, for 12–15 minutes

4 Cool on a wire rack, then store in an airtight container

Makes about 45 small biscuits

Katrina Ngaire Grigg · London E14

The 'Guess-What's-In-It' Fudge

450g (1lb) icing sugar, sifted
100g (4oz) English butter, softened
100g (4oz) Derby cheese, very finely grated
1 teaspoon vanilla flavouring
3 level tablespoons cocoa,

1 Place all the ingredients in a large bowl and mix together thoroughly using a wooden spoon

2 Lightly knead the mixture into a smooth ball

3 Divide the fudge in half and shape into 2 rolls, each about 35cm (14 inches) long. Cover with greaseproof paper, and refrigerate until quite chilled

4 Cut the rolls into even slices and the fudge is then ready to eat

Miss B. Gamble · Slough

Cheesy Monsters

4 round crusty bread rolls
198-g (7-oz) can corned beef, mashed
100g (4oz) English Cheddar cheese, grated
4 tablespoons tomato ketchup
8 olives
8 slices of gherkin
1 tomato
yeast extract

1 Open the bread rolls by cutting a zig-zag line around the front and sides of the rolls

2 Mix together the corned beef, 75g (3oz) cheese and tomato ketchup and use to fill the rolls

3 Make 2 holes in the top of each bread roll for eyes and place an olive in each

4 Stand each roll onto 2 slices of gherkin to give feet and use a piece of tomato for a tongue

5 Spread the top of each roll with a little yeast extract and stick a little of the remaining cheese to each to represent hair

Serves 4

Sidney the Snake

175g (6oz) English Cheddar cheese, grated
225-g (7½-oz) can baked beans
1 small French loaf, cut lengthways along one side
4 cooked chipolata sausages
½ cucumber, sliced
4 radishes
cocktail sticks
celery leaves

1 Mix together the grated cheese and baked beans. Use half of the mixture to fill the French loaf. Place a line of sausages along the filling and cover with the remaining filling

2 Slice across the back of the french loaf at equal intervals all the way along leaving 7·5cm (3 inches) at one end for the head. Fill each of the incisions with a slice of cucumber

3 Use 2 radishes on cocktail sticks for the eyes. Cut a slit for the mouth around the head end of the loaf and wedge it open with halved radishes

4 A sprig of celery leaves wedged between the radishes in the mouth makes an excellent 'fang'

Serves 6

Left to right: Cheesy Monsters, Treasure Chests, Sidney the Snake

Honey Bunnies

25g (1oz) English butter
15g (½oz) plain flour
2 tablespoons milk
1 tablespoon clear or thick honey
75–100g (3–4oz) Wensleydale or Lancashire cheese, grated
2 tablespoons unsweetened apple purée
2 slices of hot buttered toast or 4 warmed digestive biscuits

1 Melt the butter in a saucepan, stir in the flour and cook, stirring, for 2–3 minutes

2 Stir in the milk and honey — add slightly less than 1 tablespoon of honey if you do not want the mixture to be very sweet

3 Remove the pan from the heat and add the cheese. Mix the ingredients together thoroughly with a wooden spoon

4 Spread the apple purée thinly on the toast or digestive biscuits and spread the cheese mixture on top. Place under a hot grill until bubbling and golden. Serve immediately

Serves 2

Ms S. E. Ansell · Bristol

Cheddar Waggon Wheels

175g (6oz) plain flour
1 teaspoon baking powder
1 teaspoon dry mustard
50g (2oz) English butter
2 tablespoons milk
1 egg, beaten
175g (6oz) English Cheddar cheese, grated
200-g (7-oz) can sweetcorn, drained
salt and pepper
paprika

1 Sift flour, baking powder and mustard into a bowl. Rub in the butter until the mixture resembles fine breadcrumbs

2 Add the milk and mix to a soft dough. Turn onto a lightly floured work top and knead until smooth

3 Roll out to a rectangle approximately 23 × 27·5cm (9 × 11 inches)

4 Brush the edges with a little beaten egg

5 Spread the cheese and sweetcorn over the pastry. Season well with salt, pepper and paprika. Roll up like a Swiss roll

6 Cut into 1cm (½ inch) pieces. Place on a buttered baking sheet, cut side uppermost. Brush the dough with beaten egg and sprinkle the wheels with paprika

7 Bake 200°C (400°F), mark 6, for 15 to 18 minutes until golden brown

Makes 10–12

Mrs J. Kell · Broadstone

Treasure Chests

4 miniature brown loaves
200-g (7-oz) can luncheon meat, cubed
75g (3oz) Double Gloucester cheese
50g (2oz) cucumber, cubed
1 tablespoon salad cream
sweet corn kernels
cocktail sticks

1 Cut around the front and sides of each loaf of bread just beneath the top so that the top will lift up but is still attached. Carefully remove the soft bread from inside each loaf to leave an empty 'chest'

2 Place the cubed luncheon meat, cheese and cucumber into a bowl and mix together with the salad cream

3 Spoon the cheese mixture into the 'chests' and decorate the lids with 'jewels' of corn kernels on cocktail sticks

Do remind children to remove the jewels before eating!!

Serves 4

Basic Recipes

Shortcrust Pastry

225g (8oz) plain flour
pinch of salt
100g (4oz) English butter
2–3 tablespoons water

1 Place flour and salt into a bowl. Add the butter in pieces and rub into the flour until the mixture resembles fine breadcrumbs

2 Add the water and mix into a dough

3 Knead lightly on a floured work top and use as required

Wholemeal/Wholewheat Pastry

Use recipe for shortcrust pastry, substituting plain wholemeal flour or wholewheat flour for the plain flour

Cheese Pastry

Use recipe for shortcrust pastry with the addition of 1 level teaspoon dry mustard, 100g (4oz) English Cheddar cheese, grated, 1 egg, beaten, and sufficient water to mix into a dough.
Add the cheese after the butter has been rubbed in

White Coating Sauce

25g (1oz) English butter
25g (1oz) flour
300ml (½ pint) milk
salt and pepper

1 Place butter, flour and milk in a saucepan; heat, stirring continuously until the sauce thickens, boils and is smooth

2 Simmer for 2 minutes. Season to taste

Cheese Sauce

Add 50g (2oz) English Cheddar cheese, grated, or Lancashire cheese, crumbled, and ½ to 1 level teaspoon prepared mustard before seasoning

Index